A Hundred-Year Plan
for
Progressive Management

BOB EMILIANI, PH.D.

Improvement: A Hundred-Year Plan for Progressive Management / Bob Emiliani

Cover design by Bob Emiliani.

ISBN-13: 978-1-7320191-3-3
Library of Congress Control Number: 2020920362

1. Business 2. Improvement 3. Leadership 4. Management
5. Economics 6. Innovation 7. Technology

First Edition: November 2020

Published by Cubic LLC, South Kingstown, Rhode Island, USA.

Manufactured using digital print-on-demand technology.

CONTENTS

Dedicated to preserving the memory of human-centered management technology so that people can expand its thinking and practice in a world increasingly dominated by machine technology.

Everlasting ignorance is to condemn
before investigating.

Definitions

Progressive Management

Non-zero-sum principle-based management system featuring the application of scientific thinking to problem-solving.

Leadership

Beliefs, behaviors, and competencies that demonstrate continuous improvement and respect for people.

Classical management and associated leadership routines are defined as the inverse of the above two definitions and goes something like this:

Zero-sum principle-shifting system featuring faith and willful ignorance, informed by preconceptions to avoid improvement and evolution as times change, and disdain and disregard for people.

Preface

The aim of *Improvement* is to present a plan to carry the mindset and principal concepts and practices of progressive management forward continuously into the future, where changing times will likely demand improved leadership and management of organizations whether they are driven by machine technologies or not, and whether they are for-profit or not (see Note 1). This book seeks to correct a problem where, in the past, progressive management went dormant for periods of time. As a result, its development and evolution stalled and relinquished its role in supporting human progress in business and society. It is a situation where a step forward in progressive management thinking and practice is temporary rather than continuously building up in form and influence over long stretches of time.

Progressive management follows a pattern where new ideas are established that soon lead to strong interest among a small and dedicated group of followers. They work hard in various ways for 20, 30, or 40 years to advance progressive management. But eventually, most realize that their efforts have not produced the expected improvement. It takes a long time for people to comprehend, hazily at best, the varied phenomena that interact together to maintain the status quo. Most of these dedicated people are eventually forced to realize the truth of the famous epigram "the more things change, the more they stay the same" [1].

Nearing retirement and lacking the interest or motivation to further drive needed change, they seek other pleasures late in life and eventually pass on. Sometime later, another generation of advocates for progressive management come forward and repeats the 30-year learning cycle process. The problem, simply put, is that one generation does not build on the work of the prior generation. A generation or two skips over past achievements. They start anew as if prior problems in the efforts to advance progressive management were solved, only to find decades later that the same problems continue to exist. Efforts to improve and extend progressive management systems start and stop, thus producing a cycle of interruption instead of continuity and evolution.

What is improvement? Improvement is accurately described as "the process of a thing moving from one state to a state considered to be better, usually through some action intended to bring about that better state. The concept of improvement is important to governments and businesses, as well as to individuals" [2]. This, a seemingly harmless concept that everyone can agree on in all its applications, is surprisingly controversial when applied to the management and leadership of organizations. It is particularly offensive and harmful when those who lead organizations are asked to change their thinking and ways of doing things to affect improvement in their own work [3-6]. Significant barriers such as this must be overcome if progressive management is to creatively develop and evolve. To do that, some form of a plan is needed.

What is a plan? The word "plan" when used as a noun is commonly defined as:

- Detailed proposal for doing something
- Intention or decision about what one is going to do
- Detailed map or diagram

The word "plan" in this book is used in the sense of "an intention or decision about what one is going to do" based on the absorption of practical information to guide one's actions. It is forward-looking towards the continuous advancement of progressive management such that it studiously incorporates the lessons of the past to avoid future mistakes and to allow continuous development, evolution, and expansion of its practice. **Do not expect to see a project management plan in these pages. If you learn anything from this book it is to *not* create a project management plan**. This book is a guide towards more productive outcomes by providing descriptions of mistakes to avoid repeating and elaboration of the meaning, intent, and mindset of improvement. It illuminates more focused pathways for experimentation.

Progressive management has a long but discontinuous history, beginning in the 1500s at the Venice Arsenal and perhaps centuries earlier. Management innovations have been mostly in the form of major discrete improvements in manufacturing methods. Less common is the development of comprehensive systems of management for entire organizations, not just for production management, that represent improvement over traditional (hereafter called "classical") management practice. The source of these innovations in management systems has largely been within or in relation to manufacturing businesses. These businesses will continue to exist and remain an important source of innovative ideas for improving progressive leadership and management practice in the future. Yet, the world is changing and so the further development and evolution of progressive management will come from or be driven by other types of businesses. In particular, those that rely less on face-to-face human interaction or touch labor. These businesses and organizations, made "virtual" by way of the internet, will created demand for changes in existing systems of progressive management.

The major forms of progressive management practice in modern times are Scientific Management, Toyota's management system (TMS), and its purported generic equivalent known as Lean management (see Notes 2-4). The Scientific Management era spans the years from the late 1880s to the late 1930s, with the peak level of interest being the years between 1910 to 1930. Toyota Motor Corporation's management system began its earnest development in the years after World War II through the early 1970s when it attained more-or-less complete form. In the years since then it has continued to evolve. Studies of Toyota's management system led to the introduction in 1988 of a non-proprietary derivative version of TMS intended for use by other organizations – Lean production, later termed Lean management circa 2007 (see Note 5).

Aside from Toyota's progressive proprietary internal management practice, there was a nearly sixty-year gap between Scientific Management and Lean management. During that time, Scientific Management as a management system fell out of favor and various methods and tools were subsumed into classical management practice. This discontinuity stalled the further development and evolution of progressive Scientific Management. Fortunately, Toyota Motor Corporation allowed outside researchers to study its management practices starting around the late-1970s. This work, in addition to books written by retired Toyota executives, provided valuable insights into how progressive Scientific Management was further developed and evolved within Toyota. Unaware of the great work by Toyota managers and workers, business and industry proceeded along with classical management as the preferred system to practice.

By the mid-2000s, Lean management became a global movement, though quite small relative to the general understanding of management among business leaders and academics. In years following, interest in Lean management increased but with some limitations. First, most leaders of organizations lost interest in Lean one they realized the scope and quantity of changes need to transform from classical to Lean management. Second, and as a consequence of the first limitation, Lean management was reduced from a system to the narrow use of certain methods and tools within classical management by employees lower in the organizations – those who do actual work – to correct problems and improve their own work. Third, the appeal of Lean management resides mainly with the non-executive salaried professional staff whose influence is limited above and below their position in hierarchical organizations arranged by function [7]. Fourth, and as a consequence of the third limitation, advocates of progressive management readily compromise and conform to the norms of classical management. Fifth, Lean management, being a derivative version of Toyota's management system, faithfully follows Toyota's lead, promoting the use of various methods and tools years or decades after their use became commonplace within Toyota. In other words, Lean lacks originality and its own motive and direction for development and evolution. While Lean management is a popular offshoot of TMS and first cousin of Scientific Management, it is, in substantial ways, separate from them (see Note 6). Yet, their parallel existence leads to great confusion: Are they the same or are they different, and, if so, how, and why? Lean's path, long-term, if it survives, may be one of greater divergence from TMS or convergence to TMS. If it is the latter, then what was the point of Lean?

Consequently, the future development and evolution of progressive management best lies with Toyota and those organizations that successfully transformed to Toyota-type management systems and the associated unique ways of thinking and doing (see Note 7). Given that this is a challenging and never-ending task, one that is easily reversed back to classical management due to changes in leaders or owners, further development and evolution could again be discontinuous. For example, there is no guarantee that TMS will survive at Toyota or in organizations that have successfully transformed to Toyota-type management systems. Or, will such systems evolve into simpler, more accessible forms whose fundamental feature is the application of scientific thinking for solving leadership and management problems as well as technical (process) problems (see Note 8)? If circumstances change sufficiently and progressive management systems no longer serve a need, then they will surely fade away. If that happens, then classical management, perhaps aided by machine technologies, will continue along its long-established path – though it could evolve into a more progressive hybrid form, albeit likely still reliant on the use of discrete tools to solve problems without the required mindset (see Note 9).

There is one thing that can assure progressive management continues to move forward: people. Specifically, people who recognize there is a need for humanity to keep up with ever-changing times in relation to how people and processes, whether physical or machine, interact with one another in organizations; people who clearly recognize that such effort proceeds more efficiently and effectively by building on the work of their predecessors rather than starting from scratch; people who are willing to fight for it from a position of better knowledge of prior mistakes and ever-present opposing forces. *Improvement* hopes to serve as a guide for what has been accomplished in the past so that current and future generations can build upon the work of others. Specifically, understand their mistakes, understand the progress that has been made, and understand what is yet to be done.

In summary, this book aims to provide clear guidelines that current and future generations can put into use as they work to advance progressive management in business and other types of organizations as new machine technologies (digital and other) impinge upon people and processes. Change takes a long time; much longer than proponents of progressive management would like. But in addition to being more systematic, they must work toward outcomes based on a multi-generational (100 year) plan rather than ineffective *ad hoc* programs and disconnected activities that waste time, money, and human energy and intelligence. Hopefully, *Improvement* provides both inspiration and clarity for the challenges ahead.

Bob Emiliani
South Kingstown, Rhode Island
November 2020

Notes

1. The term "progressive" management is used to denote the opposite of traditional or "classical" management. "Progressive" meaning favoring change, improvement, and making progress, and "classical" meaning favoring the status quo. Progressive management is an encompassing term that describes the family of new management practices developed since the late 1880s: Scientific Management, Toyota management system, and Lean management. These forms of progressive management will evolve in the future to something whose form and name is presently unknown, so "progressive" is the preferred general term to describe management thinking and practice that breaks with the status quo.

2. Major works on Scientific Management include: Taylor, F.W. (1911), *Principles of Scientific Management*, Harper and Brothers, New York, New York • Cooke, M. (1913), "The Spirit and Social Significance of Scientific Management," *The Journal of Political Economy*, Vol. 21, No. 6, June, pp. 481-493 • Gilbreth, F.B. (1914), *Primer of Scientific Management*, D. Van Nostrand Co., New York, New York • Gilbreth, L.M. (1914), *The Psychology of Management*, Sturgis and Walton Co., New York, New York • Taylor, F. W. (1947), "Taylor's Testimony Before the Special House Committee" in *Scientific Management: Comprising Shop Management, Scientific Management, Testimony Before the Special House Committee*, Foreword by H. S. Person, Harper and Row Publishers, New York, New York ("Testimony of Mr. Frederick Winslow Taylor," *Hearings Before Special Committee of the House of Representatives to Investigate*

the Taylor and Other Systems of Shop Management Under Authority of H. Res. 90, Volume 3, 25 January 1912, pp. 1377-1508)

3. Major written works on Toyota's management system include: Monden, Y. (1983), *Toyota Production System: Practical Approach to Production Management*, First Edition, Engineering and Management Press, Norcross, Georgia • Lu, D. (1985), *Kanban: Just-In-Time at Toyota*, Productivity Press, Portland, Oregon, 1985 • Ohno, T. (1988), *Toyota Production System – Beyond Large-Scale Production*, Productivity Press, Portland, Oregon • Ohno, T. (1988), *Workplace Management*, Productivity Press, Cambridge, Massachusetts • Ohno, T. and Mito, S. (1988), *Just-In-Time For Today and Tomorrow*, Productivity Press, Cambridge, Massachusetts • Shinohara, I. (1988), *NPS New Production System: JIT Crossing Industry Boundaries*, Productivity Press, Cambridge, Massachusetts • Liker, J. (2004), *The Toyota Way*, McGraw-Hill, New York, New York • Kato, I. and Smalley, A. (2011), *Toyota Kaizen Methods: Six Steps to Improvement*, CRC Press, Boca Raton, Florida • Warren, M., Editor (2019), *Toyota Handbook: 1973 Edition*, Revision 0.4a, April 2019, https://bobemiliani.com/wp-content/uploads/2020/10/1973TPS-Handbook-Rev4a.pdf or https://paulakers.net/books/1973-tps-manual

4. Major written works on Lean management include: Krafcik, J.F. (1988), "Triumph of the Lean Production System," *Sloan Management Review*, Vol. 30, No. 1, pp. 41-52 • Womack, J., Jones, D., and Roos, D. (1990), *The Machine that Changed the World: The Story of Lean Production*, Rawson Associates, New York, New York • Womack, J. and Jones,

D. (1996), *Lean Thinking: Banish Waste and Create Wealth in Your Corporation*, Simon & Schuster, New York, New York

5. In its initial representation (Krafcik, J. F. (1988), "Triumph of the Lean Production System," *Sloan Management Review*, Vol. 30, No. 1, pp. 41-52) and for many years thereafter, the meaning of "Lean Production," its sameness with TMS, was assumed to be self-evident and thus went undefined. In years following, confusing and conflicting efforts were made by Lean movement leaders to signal sameness while elaborating many differences.

6. That is not to say that Lean management is without merit. Much good can come when leaders embrace Lean management, though there is much more evidence to-date of localized improvement than there is evidence of enterprise-wide transformation (see Note 7).

7. Examples of organizations that successfully transformed to Toyota-type management systems: Emiliani, B., Stec., D., Grasso, L., and Stodder, J. (2007), *Better Thinking, Better Results: Case Study and Analysis of an Enterprise-Wide Lean Transformation*, The CLBM, LLC, Wethersfield, Connecticut • Kenney, C. (2010), *Transforming Health Care: Virginia Mason Medical Center's Pursuit of the Perfect Patient Experience*, CRC Press, Boca Raton, Florida. These transformations were guided by Shingijutsu kaizen consultants. For more information on the transformation method and mindset, see these two works: Wood, R., Herscher, M., and Emiliani, B. (2015), *Shingijutsu-Kaizen: The Art of Discovery and Learning*, The CLBM, LLC, Wethersfield, Connecticut • Emiliani, B.,

Yoshino, K., and Go, R. (2015), *Kaizen Forever: Teachings of Chihiro Nakao*, The CLBM, LLC, Wethersfield, Connecticut

8. In this book, "scientific thinking" is defined as "knowledge seeking", the conscious act of "thinking that has the objective of enhancing the seekers' knowledge" which results in understanding that is useful for creative processes such as improvement. See D. Kuhn, "What is Scientific Thinking and How Does it Develop," in *Handbook of Childhood and Cognitive Development*, U. Goswami, Editor, Second Edition, Wiley-Blackwell, 2010

9. The persistent attraction to using tools to solve problems likely has its origins in human evolution, wherein tools were invented as means to aid in survival. The use of tools goes back millions of years and is presumably encoded into human thinking. In contrast, the need for humans to think in terms of systems probably occurred about 10,000 years ago when communities began to domesticate plants and animals. A more pressing need for widespread systems thinking probably occurred in the late Middle Ages and subsequently into the industrial revolution. Consequently, systems thinking in the management of people's work is a relatively new phenomenon in human history. Hence, there remains a strong tendency, perhaps an instinct, to reduce systems to discrete tools that are used as needs dictate. While progressive management advocates condemn the persistent reduction of systems to tools, the fact is that people may not be able to help themselves to see differently without strong and continuing education, guidance, and support from leaders, coaches, or mentors.

References

[1] The epigram is attributed to Jean-Baptiste Alphonse Karr circa 1848: "*Plus ça change, plus c'est la même chose.*" https://en.wikipedia.org/wiki/Jean-Baptiste_Alphonse_Karr, accessed 11 October 2020

[2] Definition of improvement is from https://en.wikipedia.org/wiki/Improvement, accessed 11 October 2020

[3] Emiliani, B. (2018), *The Triumph of Classical Management Over Lean Management: How Tradition Prevails and What to Do About It*, Cubic LLC, South Kingstown, Rhode Island

[4] Emiliani, B. (2020), *Irrational Institutions: Business, Its Leaders, and The Lean Movement*, Cubic LLC, South Kingstown, Rhode Island

[5] Emiliani, B. (2020), *Management Mysterium: The Quest for Progress*, Cubic LLC, South Kingstown, Rhode Island

[6] See Appendix I

[7] See Appendix II

Introduction

Over the past 100 years there has been much theoretical and practical study on how best to lead and manage people in organizations. This work stems from the effortless realization that there are vast opportunities to improve leadership and management. Much of these findings have been ignored by generations of leaders, or, alternatively, improvements in leadership and management practice made by one leader are either not carried forward or are reversed by the next leader. The longstanding preference among leaders is to manage people however they wish, based more on desires than study or facts. How will organizations be managed and led over the next 100 years? Will this pattern continue, or will there someday be substantive and widespread improvement? The most plausible outcome is constancy in direction, which is to lead and manage in the future as has been done in the past. While one can expect considerable advancement in machine technologies in the coming 100 years, the way that people are led and how they are deployed in organizations to do work may take the general form that exists today, much as it did 100 years earlier. Will this lack of improvement be acceptable to employees and society? Will it be appropriate given the circumstances? Will the passions and interests of those in power blind them to the need for their own progress?

At its core, progressive management seeks to transform conservative business pragmatists who prefer instincts over facts into more highly skilled leaders and managers. Top leaders' preference for instinct (e.g. "trust your gut") illuminates the social and political aspects of organizations that strongly influence decision-making. Leaders' unwavering faith in instinct is a type of superstition that allows them to dominate over the facts of a situation. It enables them to construct a more understandable and agreeable reality. Further, it allows them to feel that they are in control of complex, dynamic situations such that they are reduced to something more static and which is easier to manipulate through rudimentary comprehension and orthodox decision-making. Leading by instinct also allows leaders to project greater power through the performance of unpredictability and erratic behavior.

Instinct, born of indolence, is deployed as a tool for internal political control against those who possess the facts and thus the evidence to contravene leaders' views. Facts are an infringement on leaders' freedom to construct an altered (more successful) version of reality. It is also used to control the rate of change or depth of action taken in an organization, putting forth the ideas that neither the company nor its leaders have to evolve with the times and that harm inflicted on other people is inconsequential in relation to leaders' pursuit of their goals. Caring for others is associated with weakness and vulnerability, and therefore incongruous to the norms of leadership. The strongest leaders are those who care the least about people. Skepticism of the facts, and attacks on the facts, diminish the ability of the facts to determine policy or drive decision-making. Instinct, a seemingly supernatural ability, gives leaders the appearance of great strength whereas the facts make them look weak and powerless. As a result, obstinacy and denialism are a source of pride for leaders.

Instinct, the superhuman conquering of impersonal and disrespectful facts, is strength and thus morally praiseworthy, virtuous, and honorable. Leaders cannot be contaminated by facts unless that is their desire. Facts, and the logical arguments that they produce, are otherwise reduced to irrational feelings in self and others. To change one's thinking based on facts is a forced withdrawal, a retreat, from effective leadership. To eliminate fear in the workplace is to surrender perhaps the greatest source of leaders' power. Therefore, praise, if given, must be reversed to maintain power over others. Alternating cycles of praise and shame, flattery and abuse, and commendation and criticism generate the requisite confusion and incapacitation for critical thinking and discernment of the facts. Guilt from never being good enough or doing good enough swindles people out of their fact-based reality (see Note 1).

Subordinates and outsiders alike often stand in awe of leaders' mystical and magical powers of instinct over the facts and enthusiastically support them. They defer to authority, aid in the defense of the status quo, and dismiss mendacity – likely unaware the leader unapologetically views them with contempt. The choice they face is stark: "Like me, or else!" Yet leaders are merely doing the things they judge necessary to confirm expectations of strength and superiority. There can come a time when the facts of the situation overtake leaders' ill-constructed reality. Various monetary and non-monetary costs are incurred along the way which are largely ignored by leaders until the culmination of some form of spectacular disaster that causes great harm to the company and its stakeholders. Examples include Boeing's 737 Max aircraft [1], General Electric's downfall [2], and the daily run of significant leadership failures chronicled in *The Wall Street Journal*: e.g. Volkswagen diesel engine fraud, Wells Fargo fraud, Grenfell Tower fire, Takata defective airbags, General Motors bankruptcy, Airbus A380 blunder, Enron accounting scandal, and numerous other bankruptcies, financial frauds, quality problems, customer illnesses and fatalities, etc. (see Note 2). And there are plentiful consequential leadership failures in companies of all sizes that are never reported in the business press. They all share a common cause: the *institution of leadership* – the habits of mind; the common thinking of a group [3-6].

From the perspective of the institution of leadership, what has been described in the preceding paragraphs is entirely defect-free. Leaders, being the best, have done the best work possible. The causes of failure are habitually externalized because to take responsibility would constitute a public display of weakness and socially unacceptable degradation of leadership mores. It runs against the required ways of thinking and behaviors and is thus disallowed. Taking responsibility is reserved for lower level people, and so blame for problems must be securely attached to them. The institution of leadership requires this type of thinking and associated behaviors, and the strict avoidance of all that conflicts with it. Yet from any other perspective, this is obviously defective leadership and management of organizations (see Note 3). It is consistent over generations of leaders who unwittingly and irresponsibly sabotage the organization, in ways great and small, and disrupt the lives and livelihoods of those who depend on it. Such is the great power of the institution of leadership. The traditional antidotes to defective leadership and management are promotion, organizational restructuring, budget cutting, layoffs, and other actions that give the appearance of firm control while avoiding the actual causes of defective leadership and management. This is sedentary thinking; merely doing what other leaders do.

This is fundamentally at odds with the progressive view of management practice which demands that leaders be much more highly skilled and that the preponderance of weight be placed on facts and understanding the root causes of problems, with appropriate allowance for instinct based on experience and in consideration that knowledge can be imperfect. It has as its foundation acknowledgment of the reality that times change, and therefore systems, methods, and tools must evolve in response. Empirically, we know that fact-based decision-making produces better results in relation to the avoidance of leadership and management errors and survival of organizations. Yet, the process by which leaders rise in organizations favors the honing of social and political skills over proficient discernment of facts that result from applying scientific thinking (cause-and-effect) to the practice of management.

Progressive management begins with an assumption that leaders of hierarchical organizations can easily and somewhat quickly transform themselves from being highly skilled in social and political matters to becoming proficient in ascertaining the facts of a situation and improve their basis of decision-making. Progressive management also assumes that leaders' understanding of business and related matters can be changed by making logical technocratic and economic arguments. It further assumes that leaders want change. These and other assumptions have been proven wrong, save for the small number of leaders who fully embrace progressive management at any point in time. Overall, this confirms that the nature of leadership has long been misunderstood. Thus, there is a large gap between leaders' understanding of business and leadership and those who promote progressive management.

From the perspective of most leaders, progressive management is very unappealing because it causes them significant practical difficulties across multiple dimensions fundamental to the performance of management and leadership: economic, social, political, historical, philosophical, business, legal, and spiritual [3-6]. This constitutes an overload of change that is beyond reason.

The difficulties leaders face includes the following:

- Confounds their understanding of production, distribution, and consumption of goods and services.
- Brings dishonor to them among their peers for abandoning classical management and being different.
- Generates internal political (governance) discord.

- Undercuts their duty to preserve and uphold certain important, long-established moral principles and values.
- Threatens their understanding of leadership.
- Upsets their understanding of the role of labor.
- Requires that the ends of business can no longer be justified by the means.
- They can no longer blame other people for mistakes and problems.
- Alters legal liabilities or implied terms of contract, or the abandonment of contract terms implied by custom.
- A greater personal disgrace and loss of valor and honor than losing money or declaring bankruptcy.

It is easy to comprehend how progressive management can be viewed by leaders as that which corrupts the normative order of classical management (see Note 4).

In addition to the binding obligations of the institution of leadership, leaders have scores of preconceptions that make it difficult for them to abandon classical management and accept progressive management. These preconceptions span the categories previously identified: economic, social, political, historical, philosophical, business, legal, and spiritual. Long-established preconceptions function in combination with one another and reinforce each other (Figure I-1) such that simple but factual arguments in support of progressive management are unpersuasive to most leaders. The number of preconceptions across all categories total 120 or more, and, being interrelated, they define leaders' fundamental way of thinking – a way of thinking gained over decades of experience. The network of preconceptions provide easy justification for maintaining the status quo and avoiding progress.

Figure I-1. Closed system of recirculating archaic preconceptions that perpetuate classical management produce a preconception-based view of reality rather than a fact-based view of reality [3-6].

Furthermore, given the preconceptions of the Scholastics and subsequently the 18th century classical and 19th century neoclassical economists, where self-interest is magically transformed into a virtue that conclusively produces beneficent outcomes for society (a fallacy of composition), leaders will perceive little need for change until such time as this preconception fades into obscurity and becomes a relic of times past. When that happens, the deep and forceful social ties among leaders that bind them to their preconceptions and obligations will also weaken.

Organizations are changing and so too are employees' work and social (workplace culture) interests. As business activity increasingly shifts from person-to-person interaction to digital platforms, these intangible assets become the source of value and the driving force for virtual interaction, replacing person-to-person interaction internally and externally. Digital platforms shift the ownership of physical assets to others in a more highly distributed manner. Enterprise value is increasingly dependent on data, brands, customer base, and human capital in the forms of ideas and innovation. Growth in intellectual property drives the growth in intangible assets and a reduction in physical assets. These organizations are increasingly a greater proportion of economic output and rely on the knowledge work of employees while external resources perform person-to-person interaction if it is needed. As more organizations proceed along this trajectory, where small numbers of employees play a large role in generating enterprise value, one can expect employees to demand more from top executives in terms of leadership and management knowledge and capabilities. This might impel more leaders to advance their understanding and practice of leadership and management.

This is a time of transition from ways of thinking that are rooted in centuries past to new ways of thinking that conform to current and future needs. Dragging along old ways of thinking from the past can only impair achieving the strategy, goals, and objectives that leaders claim is essential for success. This includes not just business models, from person-to-person to digital, but how humans and machine technologies interact among and between one another. Human relations are a form of craftsmanship that needs to endure, yet classical management excels at diminishing this form of craftsmanship, reducing it to mere exchange transactions. Classical management is built on a foundation that demands such facts be ignored. Humanity needs humanism, and classical management is increasingly incapable of delivering that. Classical management coupled with virtual human interaction will prove to be unsatisfactory. Employees and society, now or in the future, will demand greater harmony rather than continued discord.

Henry Gantt, a close associate of Frederick Winslow Taylor, had a maxim that said:

> "The usual way of doing a thing
> is always the wrong way."

These words, uttered in the late 1800s, apply to any type of work including the work of leadership and management. We can take Gantt's words as a general truth or principle because any method of doing something can be improved – not once, but repeatedly. This applies to the work of laborers as well as the work of top leaders, the latter is known to be true based upon the many changes in leadership thinking and practice that are evident when leaders fully commit to progressive management [7]. That Gantt's maxim would be ignored by most leaders reflects ignorance or indifference to improving their own work, or unwavering commitment to preconceptions and the dictates of the institution of leadership which authorizes leaders to do as they please. They do not improve because they do not have to; the need, even if it were apparent, is subject to their discretion.

As time advances, leaders will become further removed from the complicated underlying digital technologies that power the enterprise, either through technical skills obsolescence, if possessed early in one's working career, or simply not understanding the machine technology to begin with due to lack of direct work experience with it. When this happens, leaders have no choice but to revert to or rely on the archaic ways of management thinking and doing that they learned from their superiors as they rose through the hierarchy. Leaders who persist with classical management when it is no longer the right thing to do create more problems – inefficient results generated in pursuit of objectives that increasingly are contrary to that which is desired. While old ways of thinking and doing passed on the job from one generation of manager to another is easily assumed to be efficient, the future need is for effectiveness which the institution of leadership as constructed over the past 350 years (and more) can no longer provide.

While leaders like to claim comprehensive credit for success, it is the working-level people to which they owe most of their success. Increasingly, non-executive employees realize this and also recognize that leaders' obligations to them are limited to minimum requirements. As a result, many other needs go unmet. Such needs can be met by transitioning to progressive management, but the usual leadership routine is to evade improvement. Commitment to *improvement evasion* reflects a culture of impunity driven by the belief that submission to rules and processes is inefficient with respect to the work of leadership and management. Within the institution of leadership, this failure to take responsibility is taken as a point of pride and free of all consequences. Yet neither sources of pride nor consequences are invariant over time.

Indifference to the needs of others exposes an underlying sociopathic behavior that is a feature of classical management and the institution of leadership, and deeply embedded in the network of preconceptions. This sets up conditions whereby employees block or withhold information. This may have been tolerable in the analog age but is less tolerable in the information age. As time passes, withholding or blocking the flow of information will become an ever-greater handicap [8]. What progressive management offers is an unblocking of human information flows, democratization of the human information system, so that people can quickly and correctly respond to changing circumstances. It seems likely that such agility will become more needed in the future, not less needed. Leaders are critical determinants as to whether information freely flows vertically and horizontally throughout the enterprise, as well as upstream to suppliers and downstream to customers.

Leaders are enablers of this priceless capability, which is likely to become more important in the future. Will they recognize human information flow as something so important that they need to abandon dozens of preconceptions rooted in classical management and the institution of leadership? Probably not, because the preconceptions and their obligations to the institution of leadership require them to deny, overlook, or ignore such things, the result of which is errors of omission and commission.

That is why devotees of progressive management must systematically push forward, one generation after the next, the mindset and methods that reflect the changes in business and social needs that began to emerge in the mid-20th century. They must, over time, work to stigmatize classical management and normalize progressive management. The former was a great achievement that worked very well for a few centuries, while the time has come for the latter.

To more effectively advance progressive management, larger numbers of people must understand more clearly the problems and pitfalls from the past and those that remain, and which will therefore plague future efforts. There must be continuous learning and improvement across generations, rather than what has happened in the past: rediscovery of old problems and pitfalls followed by inadequate problem-solving and improvements that have little or no positive effect. Discontinuous learning retards the advancement of progressive management and extends the useful life of classical management.

Figure I-2 illustrates a change that started to take place around 1990 as non-executive salaried professionals gained a better grasp of the meaning, intent, and benefits of progressive management (TMS and Lean) and associated leadership routines.

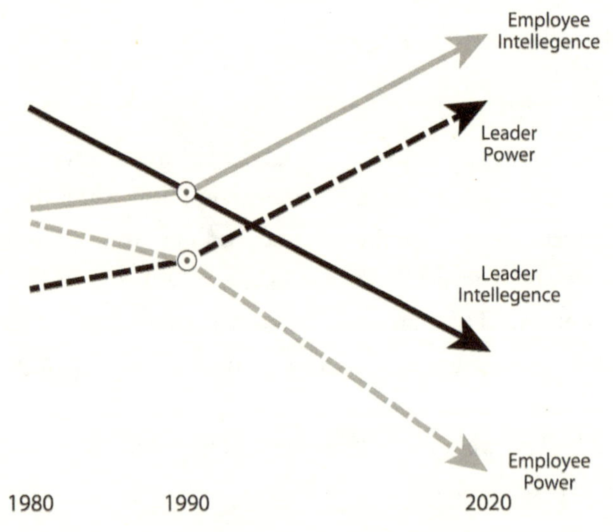

Figure I-2. The progressive management effect on employee intelligence and employee power. The gaps between leader and employee intelligence and leader and employee power have expanded over time.

Employees' intelligence of good and bad leadership and management grew while leader's intelligence of good and bad leadership and management practice declined due to unrelenting attachment to archaic preconceptions and continuing obligations to the institution of leadership. At the same time, leader power grew while employee power declined. A decline in employee power reduces their ability to recognize a problem, discover the facts, and make effective improvements. The ever-growing gaps lead to mutual dissatisfaction and mutual frustration between leaders and followers: employees do not receive the leadership acumen, management skills, and independence they demand, while leaders do not get from employees the commitment, improvement, and innovation they seek (see Note 5). As a result of leaders' determined efforts to maintain the status quo despite changing times and needs, they diminish the gains in business performance that they hope to achieve from training employees in the use of various tools and methods derived from progressive management. This contradictory outcome generates unnecessary confusion and puts in harm's way lower-level employees who are determined to make progress.

These introductory pages have spoken in broad terms and, of course, exceptions can be found to refute the characterizations made. Nevertheless, the general state of affairs is accurate and suggests a clear need for change – to break leaders' archaic preconceptions and restructure the institution of leadership and associated obligations (see Notes 6-8). While wishing for overnight success in this endeavor for change that reflects current and future needs, the course of action must be one of stepwise progress. This means building on success and, instead of ignoring failure, to carefully analyze the root causes of failure and try again and again.

For more than a century, the promoters and advocates of progressive management have made heroic efforts to bring about change. More heroism is not needed. Instead, the need is for a more systematic approach whose foundation is knowledge of the past to avoid repeating its mistakes in the future. Chapter 1 is an exposition of the conservative arguments that seek to thwart progress. Historically, these three arguments have been remarkably effective at not only thwarting progress but also entrapping those who seek change into making ineffective counterarguments. Chapter 2 discusses the most important mistakes made in efforts to advance Scientific Management and, fifty years later, Lean management. There is also a brief review of the creative decades-long development of Toyota's management system and how this should be the basis for advancing progressive management.

Chapter 3 describes the basic mindset that brings forth continuous improvement in ways that respect people's work and personal lives. It describes important features that are missing or underrepresented in the literature. Also included are two research papers. Appendix I examines means and ends in classical and contemporary systems of progressive management using a Western philosophical framework to help people imagine new strategies and tactics to gain wider acceptance for progressive management. Appendix II provides an analytical framework to understand and interpret the social status phenomenon associated with the Lean movement which has had a negative effect on the advancement of progressive management.

In summary, the focus of this book is this simple problem statement:

What methods will result in wider acceptance for progressive management?

The solution to this problem is unknown. Therefore, one must not assume they know the answer. Instead, a community of interested persons must generate and test many new ideas and learn from the various outcomes (see Note 9). It is hoped that this volume will help ground interested parties in a base of knowledge that they can systematically built upon to advance progressive management over the next 100 years.

Notes

1. Leaders "control the narrative," as the saying goes, which means they control the human information system as to what is real and what is not. Employees look to leaders as the authority on reality (truth) which they largely accept because they are part of, and want to remain with, the in-group – employees of the company. By default, workers are predisposed to trusting their leaders. They must do so because their lives and livelihoods depend on it, and because their peers trust the top leader and agree with their telling of reality. This forms a general agreement as to what constitutes reality, one that is hostile to out-groups who challenge that reality. Internal advocates of progressive management, who seek to break the status quo that the in-group cherishes (called "system justification"), are one such out-group. Those in the in-group think and act in homogenous ways which supplies the evidence needed that their understanding of reality is rational. It has the apparent benefit of reducing uncertainty but instead generates greater uncertainty and chaos because facts are ignored to greater or lesser extents. As a result, problems in organizations exist as chronic, rather than acute ailments. People accept chronic problems as "just the way things are," thus cementing their understanding of reality as accurate and valid.

2. Since 2004, the author has taught a unique course that formally analyzes failures in executive decision-making using a method developed by the author. One of the many important findings from analyzing over five dozen failures

is that top leaders are remarkably prone to making "penny-wise, pound-foolish" decisions. For example, decisions made to save money in the development of a new product often end up costing the company five or ten times the anticipated savings. Other findings reveal the specific cognitive biases and forms of illogical thinking that lead to faulty decision-making. It turns out that the thing which managers are the most confident about – analysis, logical thinking, and decision-making – are the things they should be the least confident about. Management information processing is highly error-prone and must be improved. Archaic preconceptions and the institution of leadership are major contributors to faulty executive decision-making.

3. Leadership is commonly understood to be a defect-free activity, when it is in fact a defect-filled activity. For proof of this, see Emiliani, B. (2015), *Speed Leadership: A New Way to Lead for Rapidly Changing Times*, The CLBM LLC, Wethersfield, Connecticut.

4. Today, we understand the word "corruption" to mean actions that are dishonest or fraudulent. Etymologically, however, the word "corruption" means (in Middle English) to "break," "debase," "alter" (in an unfavorable way), or "destroy." Classical management, as it is understood by generations of top business leaders for more than 200 years, represents a preexisting normative order — one which most CEOs in modern times are very pleased with. Progressive management advocates for a type of leadership and management restructuring that breaks, debases, alters, or destroys classical management. Therefore, progressive

management represents corruption of the much-loved classical management. In addition, progressive management corrupts the preexisting social hierarchy and political order that leaders view as necessary for personal and business success. To suggest to leaders that progressive management is necessary – for any reason – is taken as personal insults and threatens to corrupt their business worldview. Furthermore, bids to advance progressive management by those lower in the hierarchy is inherently corrupt because they are lower in status. What promoters of progressive management see as beneficial and necessary, most leaders see as corruption of the existing order and they will fight to prevent corruption of classical management from taking place and preserve the purity, value, and traditions of classical management and leadership.

5. Gallup's Employee Engagement survey shows that employee engagement has been stagnant or decreasing since the late 1990s in the United States and other developed countries. According to Gallup "managers account for at least 70% of the variance in employee engagement scores." This suggests workers are frustrated with their managers and top leaders, and that the expectations of younger generations are increasingly not being met as they enter the workforce. See https://www.gallup.com/workplace/229424/employee-engagement.aspx and https://www.gallup.com/workplace/238079/state-global-workplace-2017.aspx, accessed 16 October 2020

6. It appears that merely being in a leadership position alters one's thinking in ways that align with scores of

preconceptions and the institution of leadership. This includes the inability to see facts or take responsibility for problems. Efforts to present the facts are taken as insults to one's leadership and management skills, such that one fact equals one insult, five facts equals five (or more) insults, and so on. This seeming correspondence foretells the harm that subordinates may unwittingly run into. As for avoiding responsibility, it is well-known that leaders externalize responsibility and accountability to others to the maximum extent that they can get away with, because to take responsibility is to acknowledge weakness and make one's weakness visible to all others. Facts and responsibility are threats, wherein the first instinct of leaders is to metaphorically isolate themselves or flee from them as if they were a dangerous bacteria or highly contagious virus. In a weird way, it may also be true that leaders beholden to classical management cannot accept responsibility because they sense being immersed in a no-win situation, unable to navigate the dynamic interplay between self-regarding and other-regarding – so they capitulate to the former.

7. Art Byrne, former CEO of The Wiremold Company, called the famous Shingijutsu kaizen consultant, Chihiro Nakao, an "insultant" because Mr. Nakao would criticize managers for the poor shape the business was in under their leadership. Mr. Nakao would bluntly point out the facts of the situation: "Why are you doing this? Throw this out! Get rid of this! Close the warehouse! You don't know anything." He would "fire" managers when they made excuses. The purpose of the insults and firings was to shock managers out of complacency, challenge them to abandon their

preconceptions, advance their understanding and practice of management, and develop their skills as leaders. Over time, Mr. Nakao delivered the facts a bit more softly, but he never hesitated to get in your face if you made excuses.

8. One of the enduring paradoxes is managers' desire for employees to be critical thinkers. Managers persistently say they favor employees who possess this valuable skill, taught from grade school through graduate school. Yet facts, generally the result of critical thinking, are often unwelcomed by managers. Of course, one important feature of the institution of leadership is that it is both acceptable and respectable for leaders to be inconsistent (and hypocritical, when needed). It is therefore acceptable and respectable for business leaders to criticize higher education for not teaching people the skills needed for employment such as critical thinking. Is that not a fact? Further, one notices that top leaders rarely visit the locations where actual work is performed, preferring instead to isolate themselves in executive offices. Direct contact with workers raises the unpleasant, if not offensive, possibility that they will come face-to-face with the facts which will disrupt their theoretical understanding of workers and the work – and might create work for them to do such as correct chronic problems. These too are facts.

9. Much as Henry Gantt is to be loved, the outcome of this book *must not* be the creation of Gantt Charts. Learn more about Henry Gantt, see the 1934 biography by L.P. Alford, *Henry Laurence Gantt: Leader in Industry*, The American Society of Mechanical Engineers, New York, New York.

References

[1] Majority Staff of the Committee on Transportation and Infrastructure (2020), "Final Committee Report: The Design, Development & Certification of the Boeing 737 MAX," The House Committee on Transportation and Infrastructure, September, https://transportation.house.gov/committee-activity/boeing-737-max-investigation, accessed 12 October 2020

[2] Gryta, T. and Mann, T. (2020), *Lights Out: Pride, Delusion, and the Fall of General Electric*, Houghton Mifflin Harcourt, New York, New York

[3] Emiliani, B. (2018), *The Triumph of Classical Management Over Lean Management: How Tradition Prevails and What to Do About It*, Cubic LLC, South Kingstown, Rhode Island

[4] Emiliani, B. (2020), *Irrational Institutions: Business, Its Leaders, and The Lean Movement*, Cubic LLC, South Kingstown, Rhode Island

[5] Emiliani, B. (2020), *Management Mysterium: The Quest for Progress*, Cubic LLC, South Kingstown, Rhode Island

[6] See Appendix I

[7] See for example, Emiliani, B., Stec., D., Grasso, L., and Stodder, J. (2007), *Better Thinking, Better Results: Case Study and Analysis of an Enterprise-Wide Lean Transformation*, The CLBM LLC, Wethersfield, Connecticut • Kenney, C. (2010),

Transforming Health Care: Virginia Mason Medical Center's Pursuit of the Perfect Patient Experience, CRC Press, Boca Raton, Florida.

[8] Emiliani, B. (2015), *Speed Leadership: A New Way to Lead for Rapidly Changing Times*, The CLBM, LLC Wethersfield, Connecticut

1
Arguments Against Progressive Management

Arguments Against Progressive Management

The Introduction explained in rough outlines why leaders resist or reject progressive management. But there are many more details that readers must learn about classical management if they wish to make progressive management more common in organizations. A full description of the institution of leadership – the "lay of the land" – can be found in References 1-4. This is necessary reading because, unfortunately, leaders will not fully explain their dislike for progressive management as described in those works because it gives away too many of their deepest secrets. Instead, leaders will justify their dislike for progressive management using three rudimentary, if not simplistic, high-level arguments: Jeopardy, Perversion, and Futility [5].

These powerful arguments are put forward to conserve the current state; to preserve the status quo by fending off progressive thinking and practices; to put progressive management into arrears and, eventually, discredit it. These three arguments have existed for centuries. They remain useful because it produces the desired results — to slow down change, stop change, or even go backwards. Advocates of progressive management must understand these overused arguments so they can refute them and be aware of traps that they may inadvertently set for themselves when they make counterarguments.

It is important to recognize that both the allies and enemies of progressive management are good people putting forth arguments that align with their deepest personal and work-related beliefs. Their arguments reflect reality as they see it, though not necessarily unbiased or untainted by cynicism or free of ulterior motives. One thing to consider as you read this Chapter is that if progressive management were seen as a large threat by business leaders, you would see the three arguments Jeopardy, Perversion, and Futility fully, forcefully, and consistently deployed by CEOs, politicians, conservative think tanks, etc., in the media and elsewhere.

The fact that these arguments remain somewhat weak and limited in their deployment shows that progressive management is not yet seen as a significant threat to those in power and the normative order of leadership and business. For over 30 years, leaders have been able to very effectively control the intrusion of progressive (i.e. Lean) management into classical management by limiting its influence to some tools they require lower level employees to use – and thus retarding the advancement of leadership and management practice.

The three arguments, which you are no doubt familiar with to some degree, follow a logical sequence in their deployment by those who are hostile to change and improvement. While the arguments are rudimentary, they are highly effective and can be deployed *ad infinitum*, drawn upon whenever needed, as shown by the circular arrow shown in Figure 1-1. It shows the three arguments, the sequence in which they are deployed, and the fact that the same arguments are reused or recycled time and time again because they are so effective as shaping the opinions of people who prefer to maintain the status quo or who are uncertain about change, whether it is worth the effort, or whether it will lead to actual change (versus appearance of change).

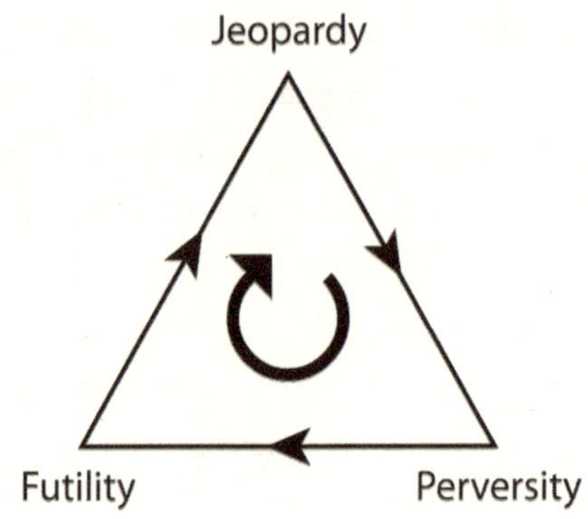

Figure 1-1. The reactionary rhetoric loop. The sequence of arguments begins with Jeopardy, proceeds to Perversity, and concludes with Futility – until the process begins anew based on the existing threat, its modification, or a new threat.

It begins with Jeopardy, which is a prediction that bad things will happen if progressive management were to replace classical management. The amount of harm is always exaggerated for greater effect. Next comes the Perversity argument, which comes from observation, where change has resulted in outcomes that are opposite of what was intended. Lastly, the Futility argument, whose formulation is based on the production of results over a long period of time, argues that no real change has been achieved despite great effort, and so there is no point in continuing further to seek ameliorative change. The three arguments utilize skepticism and sarcasm as effective rhetorical devices. The arguments are presented in ways that seek to undermine or reverse progress. Embedded within them is deception in the form of illogical thinking (e.g. straw man, false assumptions, abuse of expertise, avoiding the force of reason, false dilemma, special pleading, expediency) [7], and confirmation bias (e.g. anchoring, sunk cost, confirming evidence, status quo). The three arguments are deployed as follows:

Jeopardy Argument

Progressive management is a leap that will bring disastrous consequences. It will (in various ways) change things for the worse instead of for the better.

While such deductive arguments are entirely speculative, they carry great weight because of the consequences that failure can bring. Progressive management, lacking cookbook standardization for transition from classical management, is filled with many different types of risks and challenges – especially when unskilled managers lead the transformation – and so the likelihood of many failures large and small is high.

In classical management, people get blamed for problems. Thus, problems are to be avoided if one hopes to advance within the hierarchy or remain employed. A familiar prediction is how improvements in production will upset downstream processes such as the ability to grow sales or satisfy customer demand; essentially, the animating concern is "we will lose more than we gain." Other familiar predictions include the shift to progressive management will cost too much, it will take too long, and it will endanger previous accomplishments or recent gains in performance. Leaders will say "the time is not right," "we are not ready for progressive management," "we're too busy," or "progressive management is no longer relevant." Many types of excuses will be made to assure no action is taken.

The Jeopardy argument against progressive management comes not only from the top leaders of a company, but from middle managers and supervisors who reiterate the thinking of their superiors. It also comes from workers on the frontlines. They will join in the predictions and say that progressive management will dehumanize them, speed them up, and burn them out, take away their knowledge and creativity, and cost them their job. In addition, external stakeholders (e.g. politicians, reporters, etc.) may argue against progressive management by citing an anticipated reduction in leaders' autonomy – a customary benefit that has been enshrined into law in some countries. Several sources citing the same or similar Jeopardy arguments can appear to form a consensus of opinion which authenticates and validates the argument as an unbiased truth. Defeat of progressive management may thus occur before having even been started.

Perversity Argument

Progressive management made existing conditions worse – it backfired.

Rather than being a remedy to improve, progressive management was injurious to the current ways of doing things. An example that was extensively reported in the business press in 2020 pertains to Just-in-Time. JIT "inventory management practices" failed when needed most during the COVID-19 crisis. It is irrelevant that reporters did not understand JIT, that the stories were inaccurate and misleading, that most business leaders misunderstand JIT, or that most companies practice JIT incorrectly. Rather than determine the root causes of these problems, the only clear and sensible solution is to shift away from JIT "inventory management practices" to "stockpiling months, rather than weeks" of material. This creates new demand for additional warehouse and distribution capacity which other businesses, following the innately correct logic of their customers, are delighted to satisfy.

Many people have heard or witnessed other examples where progressive management went wrong and caused various forms of confusion, errors, delays, and re-work – a singular or chain of unintended consequences contrary to the goals of progressive management – made matters worse. Progressive management's perverse effect is "change for the worse," rather than "change for the better, which in this argument is seen as predictable.

The perversity argument is easy to deploy because observations of something new and challenging that is attempted by inexperienced managers is certain to be fraught with problems that can, almost effortlessly, be shown to be a failure in part or whole. Advocates for maintaining the status quo are typically very vocal and will be quick to point out the perverse effects, repeatedly.

Futility Argument

Progressive management failed to deliver the promised improvements.

There are few strong examples of the transformation from classical management to progressive management, and thus very few leaders who have led such transformations. The best that progressive management has done in most organizations has been to produce some cosmetic changes while the underlying systems and ways of thinking and doing things remain largely, if not wholly, unchanged. Hence the negatively biased epigram "the more things change, the more they stay the same."

Art Byrne, a former CEO who has led many transformations, tells leaders that "transformation" means "everything must change." These words may do more to assure that everything stays the same than Art and others realize – a perverse effect, to be sure, one that reinforces both the futility and jeopardy arguments. The words, "everything must change" is dissonant to the ears of leaders, most of whom seek no such comprehensive change in leadership and management practice. In fact, they actively seek to avoid change of such great magnitude.

In most organizations, the changes that come from progressive management are not, in fact, the deep change as sought by the proponents of progressive management. Their desire is to elevate workers and make use of their intelligence and creativity to develop themselves and advance the interests of the company, yet the highly structured normative order of leadership and business is driven to ensure that workers (the majority) cannot disturb the power, rights, privileges, and decision-making authority of leaders (the minority). Leaders' continued dominance and disdain for relinquishing power, even small bits of power (see Note 1), dooms most attempts for transformation.

Every so often the business press carries stories about large companies whose best, most productive manufacturing facilities or service centers were closed by company leaders. This outcome demoralizes employees, and generally any worker who reads the news, and causes them to ask: "Is it even worth trying?" Human thinking and labor are precious resources that few people are inclined to willingly expend on effort that is judged to be futile. Employees who make or join futility arguments can be very persuasive at re-directing their peers to existing work that is more productive and rewarding.

One can see that these three arguments are based on speculation and selective use of evidence to subvert efforts to disturb the status quo. In essence, they are political arguments, ones that are highly effective at thwarting improvement in management thinking and practice. The Jeopardy argument is essentially fortune-telling, wherein people comprehend predictions as mystical human abilities that are worthy of consideration. Such visions are held in high esteem and believed to be true even if they are later proven to be wrong. The Perversity argument is the cherry-picking of information that supports one's view while ignoring information that contradicts it. When something is new, such as progressive management, people are more inclined to believe negative information and outcomes over positive ones. The Futility argument supports people's preference to keep doing in the future what they have done in the past – to maintain the status quo because results currently achieved are good enough.

These three arguments, Jeopardy, Perversity, and Futility, and their embedded false or exaggerated claims are effective at contaminating the process for making progress and reducing trust in the people who advocate for progressive management. They then fall into the trap of continually trying to prove themselves and their case for progressive management, usually to no avail. These three arguments are also effective at reducing confidence that improvement is within easy reach. Instead, improvement is made out to be a distant and impractical dream. The lessening of trust and confidence sets up conditions for entrenched tribalism and unproductive protracted us-versus-them conflicts. Each side becomes preoccupied with carrying on the fight while both time and opportunity slip away. Importantly, the lessening of trust and confidence also impairs learning and innovation that will improve the human condition as times change.

What can be done to refute or circumvent these arguments? The most likely action that progressive management advocates will take is to make the same three simplistic arguments but from the opposite direction and trap themselves into a stalemate. Opposing arguments utilize certainty and moral indignation as ineffective rhetorical devices, and may be expressed as follows (see Note 2):

Jeopardy Counterargument

The future is grim. Continuing to do things as they have always been done will make things worse. Lean will strengthen, not weaken, business and society. The company will be more competitive and survive. Progressive management will save the company. It will repair and invigorate capitalism. If you don't adopt Progressive management, the consequences will be disastrous. Things will not improve if we don't try. Inaction carries great danger.

Perversity Counterargument

We have seen the results. The way things have been done in the past yield uneven outcomes for people; there are too many losers. Economic preconceptions serve the rich. Globalization backfired. Workers are asked to think but they are rewarded only for doing. Employees have become alienated from their work and their employers. Classical management has failed and must be replaced from the ground up with progressive management.

Futility Counterargument

Classical management cannot be improved. It delivers only for shareholders and not for stakeholders. Stakeholder capitalism cannot function under classical management – instead it requires progressive management. Bad things will keep happening if we do not embrace change. We cannot keep up with the times when things remain the same. The status quo cannot compete with evolution and humanity's desire for change.

The likely effect of these three counterarguments is no change. The opposing arguments cancel each other out, but easily favor those aligned with the status quo because doing nothing is easier than doing something. Preserving the current state and the normative order of leadership and business, while dissatisfying to some is ultimately accepted.

So, what can advocates of progressive management do to confront the three arguments against transformation? From Toyota [7] and their practice of kaizen we learn a way of thinking about problems that can erode or blunt – though perhaps not defeat – these arguments:

Demystify the Jeopardy Argument

Jeopardy Argument: The cost of transformation will outweigh its benefits. **Counterargument**: These are predictions. Stop making predictions. Don't brainstorm. Instead, try it out for yourself and see.

Rectify the Perversity Argument

Perversity Argument: Progressive management produced the opposite results. **Counterargument**: You tried it out and it did not work. Don't give up. Try again and keep trying. Be creative and continuously improve your methods to achieve the intended results.

Repudiate the Futility Argument

Futility Argument: Progressive management failed to produce the intended result. **Counterargument**: Approach the work with optimism. Accept the challenge with creativity and energy. Build trust and work as a team.

These counterarguments, rooted in humanism instead of the supernatural and mundane, discredit the Jeopardy, Perversity, and Futility arguments. They suggest that humans have far greater ability to use intelligence to do good things than is normally recognized, and that by working together individuals, organizations, and society can benefit. The counterarguments also subtly imply that the people who make such arguments are parochial, indolent, and self-interested. These are not characterizations that people, especially leaders, wish to be known by. Some leaders may be moved by this or the threat of self-inflicted embarrassment or humiliation.

Of course, the counterarguments will be more forceful if one is a position of power, which often is not the case. Counterarguments can easily be perceived by those in power to be unwarranted and disrespectful. Even the most respected top leaders of transformed businesses have great difficulty convincing their peers of the merits of transitioning to progressive management. They will push only so far and then give up or wait for another day.

Furthermore, the three arguments against progressive management are premised on the high value attributed to the normative order of leadership and business as seen by business leaders, politicians, and society (see Note 3). But this premise will not have a hold on people indefinitely. When it falters, there will be an opening for wider acceptance of progressive management. But that could be far into the future (see Note 4). In the meantime, it is wise to learn the lessons of the past so that they are not repeated in the future.

Notes

1. See Preface, Note 9. The human desire for power may have similar evolutionary origins; to have a sense of control over various types of human and non-human threats.

1. In his work, the author (Emiliani) has made the same or similar Jeopardy, Perversity, and Futility counterarguments as the ones presented on pages 35 and 36.

2. Whether leaders like it or not, corporations, especially large ones, become deeply integrated into society, in part by providing the public with goods and services. The self-interested pursuit of profits can undercut obligations to society that are created due to the very existence of the corporation. From the early 1980s through 2020, the obligations of corporations to society has gone largely unrecognized by most leaders of large companies.

3. In the interim, alternate paths can be explored. For example, leaders and followers could negotiate a practical solution that brings changes that are acceptable to both parties. What would precipitate such good-faith negotiation is unknown. A proposed negotiated solution was presented in the book *The Triumph of Classical Management Over Lean Management: How Tradition Prevails and What to Do About It.* It is called iMaP – "Improved Management Practice" – whose intent is to get both parties to agree on a small set of changes designed to be mutually beneficial. Perhaps that can be a productive way forward in the evolution of progressive management. What other solutions can you think of?

References

[1] Emiliani, B. (2018), *The Triumph of Classical Management Over Lean Management: How Tradition Prevails and What to Do About It*, Cubic LLC, South Kingstown, Rhode Island

[2] Emiliani, B. (2020), *Irrational Institutions: Business, Its Leaders, and The Lean Movement*, Cubic LLC, South Kingstown, Rhode Island

[3] Emiliani, B. (2020), *Management Mysterium: The Quest for Progress*, Cubic LLC, South Kingstown, Rhode Island

[4] See Appendix I

[5] Hirschman, A. (1991), *The Rhetoric of Reaction: Perversity, Futility, Jeopardy*, Belknap Press, Boston, Massachusetts.

[6] McInerny, D. (2005), *Being Logical: A Guide to Good Thinking*, Random House, New York, New York

[7] "The Toyota Way 2001," (2001), Internal Document, Global Human Resources Division, Toyota Motor Corporation, Toyota City, Japan, April

2
Learn from the Past

Learn from the Past

The typical progressive management devotee enters the field through an uptake of current knowledge of the subject. If they are dedicated, they will work years to absorb the current knowledge that is available in its many and varied forms. At the same time, they will put into practice whatever training they have received and knowledge that they have gained from current books and other sources. While they may be filled with current knowledge (see Appendix II), they likely possess little or no knowledge of the history of progressive management – the few successful outcomes and the many mistakes made by those before them. They will assume that whatever problems existed in the past are not relevant in their current time. They will assume successful outcomes in the past have led to successful outcomes in their current time. They will further assume that all the mistakes of the past have been corrected and the path to future success is, therefore, sure to be easier. For some, ignorance of this is a point of pride, learning from experience is the only thing of worth, and books have nothing to offer except income for their authors.

The situation is not much better for the people who lead progressive management movements. They too know little of the past, and what they do know likely includes misunderstandings as well as many factual errors. Yet these people are influential; their lack of knowledge of the past, misunderstandings, and errors is highly effective at shaping the knowledge and thinking of their followers. Invariably, progressive management movement leaders derive income from their followers in various ways. Taking their money should be some motivation to learn the facts of the past and convey accurate information so that their time and lives are not wasted. Such work and dedication to one's craft would be ongoing. Yet this plainly is too much to ask to those whose business it is to promote and sell progressive management.

While the aphorism "Those who cannot remember the past are condemned to repeat it" [1] can be accurate, more or less so, it provides little motivation to leaders or followers to study the past to avoid repeating mistakes. Additionally, there is much truth to the adage that people learn by making mistakes. But one must consider whether learning in a professional (work or business) context is efficient or effective if one assumes that current problems are unique and thus unrelated to the past. Admittedly, it can be challenging to find relevant information, but it is also easier than ever given the internet and the digitization of books and periodicals from the past. The bigger difficulty is sorting good and useful information from that which is less relevant or useless. That is where this book hopes to offer some measure of benefit.

There is also a broad-based inability for devotees of progressive management to distinguish between self-interested or inexperienced promoters and hucksters and those who possess the practical knowledge of how to achieve change in the workplace and among the executive team. Glossy sales pitches are often much more influential than long track records of knowledge, wisdom, and improvement results, which is the presumed reason for having interest in progressive management. Opposite that is an inability among the progressive management leaders and prominent influencers to accept criticism of their work and clearly acknowledge missteps and mistakes – which, if done, is a decade or more after the fact and any corrections made are often behind the times or otherwise largely inadequate or ineffective. The distributed tasks of saving face and defending one's heroes takes on an importance greater than the advancement of progressive management itself. Consequently, progressive management is often viewed by outsiders as a cult or religion, one that offers far more than it is able to deliver. This marginalization is wholly self-inflicted and the impulse to avoid it is continuously absent.

Needless repetition of past mistakes inhibit progress – not just progress itself, but, importantly, the pace of progress. Those who stand against progress, who see no need to keep up with the times or who may even prefer reverting to past times, are happy to see those in favor of progress struggle and achieve little or nothing during their professional lifetimes. They have been handed a gift like none other, one that requires no effort on their part to obtain the result that they desire most: maintain the status quo and its associated power, rights, and privileges. Those who failed can, at minimum, say they learned something. And perhaps they even had a good time. But the fruits of their efforts, in general, either did not blossom or were eventually reversed by subsequent leaders intent on preserving classical management. These leaders deny the need for change while progressive management leaders and practitioners consistently underestimate their determination to keep things as they are or ensure that they can limit or modulate progress and the rate of change.

Figure 2-1 illustrates how classical management and progressive management are on different paths. The longer path belongs to classical management and the more recent path belongs to progressive management. While classical management is depicted as unchanged over time, it does in fact undergo some adaptation as times change. However, the social habits of thought that are in control of those changes date back thousands of years [2-4]. These habits of thought are informed by scores of economic, social, political, historical, philosophical, legal, business, and spiritual preconceptions that are seen as having immense current and endless future value. Its simplistic intellectual heritage, if one can even call it "intellectual" (see Note 1), is *de jure* – by right, the leaders' right to accept or reject change as they decree. Hence, the need to vigorously defend against incursions whether they are small or large. This results in a continuity to classical management thinking and practice that excludes progress which will be needed as times change and as people's wants and needs change.

Progressive management comes from a different, non-atavistic, rigorous intellectual heritage whose fundamental feature is improvement; that of engineering and science – the domain of experimentation, observation, and facts. While it is also subject to the same array of preconceptions, the acceptance of the scientific method, structured or trial-and-error experimentation, observation, logic, facts, and the

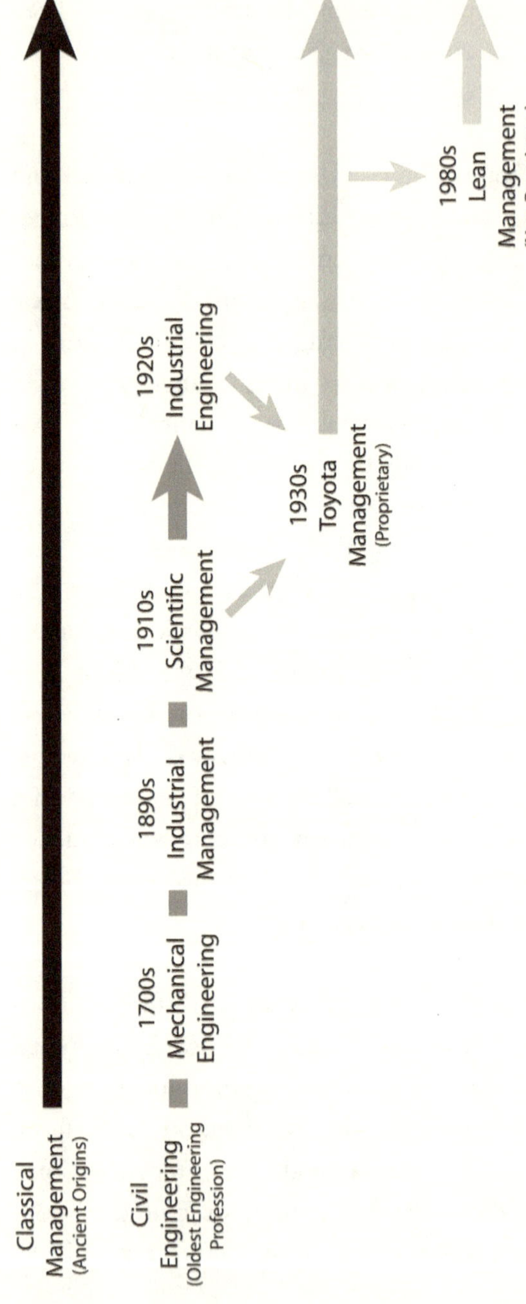

Figure 2-1. Classical management, with ancient origins and rooted in preconceptions, and the evolution of progressive management (proprietary and generic versions), more recent in origin and rooted in perceptions (engineering practice and scientific thinking). Time not to scale.

the creation of new technologies disables otherwise paralyzing economic, social, political, historical, philosophical, legal, business, and spiritual preconceptions. Therefore, the lineage of progressive management thinking and practice fully accepts as fact the need for and desirability of change to improve the human experience – continuous change, with instinct being anemic as a controlling force (see Notes 2 and 3). As such, leadership is flexible compared to the authoritarian disposition of classical management. Thus, progressive management is *avant-garde* (ahead of the keepers of tradition), at the leading edge of innovation in management thinking and practice.

Despite the focus on problem-solving and the primacy of facts, the promotion and advancement of progressive management has been deeply marred and tarnished by numerous missteps and mistakes that are seen as better to ignore and move on rather than to thoroughly understand and correct (see Note 4). The following pages present the principal mistakes that have been made in the past or continue to be made, and which, to some degree, have lessened the appeal of progressive management to those committed to classical management. These constitute ongoing opportunities for improvement and to correct chronic weaknesses in the understanding, promotion, and practice of progressive management. Avoiding or correcting these mistakes may help pave the way for expanded acceptance of progressive management, as a time may come when leaders will face the need to take a greater interest in progressive management. Depending upon the mistake, it can be corrected beforehand or when needed.

Scientific Management Mistakes

1. **Giving the System a Name.** To distinguish itself from classical management, there seems to always be a need to give a new and specific name to progressive management. Prior to being named "Scientific Management," the name given by Taylor's colleagues was "The Taylor System" in honor of its principal creator, Frederick Winslow Taylor. But Taylor never called it that, preferring "shop management" instead. He did not like naming it after a person because he was just one of many who created it and protested such branding [5]. Attorney and future U.S. Supreme Court justice Louis Brandeis, along with Henry Gantt and Frank Gilbreth, renamed it "Scientific Management," thinking that this would carry greater significance in an important court case. Taylor approved of this term believing that it would gain wider acceptance among business owners and managers.

   Despite that rationale, the name "Scientific Management" was an accurate description for the application of scientific thinking to the practice of management. The name, while apt, suggested to business leaders that they were non-scientific in their management, which, no doubt, was understood implicitly and explicitly as an insult to their leadership acumen and management skills. One could name Scientific Management "Free Money," "Free Love," or "P400" and there would be few takers because progressive management so thoroughly disrupts leaders' worldview (their preconceptions). The name, the branding of the product, becomes a new and difficult problem to contend with. *In summary, the mistake was to give it a name* – though "progressive management" would be very problematic to most business leaders even if it were nameless (see Note 5).

2. **Making Ineffective Arguments.** Initial efforts to appeal to business leaders to replace classical management with Scientific Management centered on logical technical arguments. These were the arguments that the developers of Scientific Management understood best and therefore believed to be the most compelling arguments to make to leaders. These logical technical arguments were successful in some cases, but that may have been due to other reasons such as a combination of interest in the new, a willingness to experiment, or personal friendship. The actual reasons why a few dozen early adopters accepted Scientific Management as Taylor and his team envisioned it is unknown.

   Soon it became apparent that despite the public reporting of good results, most leaders were uninterested in Scientific Management. Taylor and his team stuck with logical technical arguments, but others did not. The emerging field of management consulting led to a proliferation of "efficiency engineers" who would help companies improve operations using diluted forms of Scientific Management (See Note 6). They proffered a more emotionally appealing pecuniary argument – higher profits (wealth accumulation for owners) – not dry technical arguments. This argument appealed to a greater number of business leaders, yet still small in relation to the overall number of businesses. Most business leaders preferred to run their organizations as they saw fit and maintained their right to determine which methods or tools were appropriate for use given their (assumed to be) unique circumstances. *In summary, the mistake was to focus on technical, and later, economic arguments, because neither produced the desired results of abandoning classical management nor improving efficiency.*

3. **Dramatizing the Magnitude of Change.** In his book 1911 *The Principles of Scientific Management*, Taylor said [6]:

   > "…the really great problem involved in a change from the management of 'initiative and incentive' to scientific management consists in a complete revolution in the mental attitude and the habits of all of those engaged in the management…"

   In his 1912 testimony to Congress defending Scientific Management, Taylor said [7]:

   > "Now, in its essence, scientific management involves a complete mental revolution on the part of the workingman engaged in any particular establishment or industry—a complete mental revolution on the part of these

> men as to their duties toward their work, toward their fellow men, and toward their employers. And it involves the equally complete mental revolution on the part of those on the management's side—the foreman, the superintendent, the owner of the business, the board of directors — a complete mental revolution on their part as to their duties toward their fellow workers in the management, toward their workmen, and toward all of their daily problems. And without this complete mental revolution on both sides scientific management does not exist. That is the essence of scientific management, this great mental revolution."

Taylor was correct in his characterization of the extent of personal and business change that Scientific Management required. The "mental revolution" meant both managers and workers had to abandon many of their most dearly held preconceptions. However, this requirement was toxic to most leaders despite any gains that might be achieved due to Scientific Management. Most business leaders are conservative; they are far more interested in maintaining the status quo and completely disinterested in revolution of any kind. They did not want to undergo a "great mental revolution," nor did they want their workers to undergo a "great mental revolution." That is why efficiency engineers were more successful in gaining acceptance for their proposals for improvement than Taylor and his colleagues (see Notes 6 and 7).

The persistent characterizations of Scientific Management as a "great mental revolution" and "complete mental revolution" was seen as highly undesirable, for myriad reasons [2-4], to those who lead organizations. Additionally, the fact that change would take four or five years did not help matters (see Note 6) given that expedient conduct (pragmatism based on self-interest) is the controlling force in the thinking and practice of classical management [8]. *In summary, the mistake was to characterize the change in management thinking and practice as something grandiose, immense, and lofty.*

4. **Not Understanding How Leaders Think.** Taylor and his colleagues, as well as the efficiency engineers, assumed they understood the mindset of leaders: their passions and interests, their likes and dislikes, and their wants and needs. Some, like Taylor, had been corporate executives earlier in their careers and most of his colleagues regularly interacted with top leaders. Yet, their great excitement over the new system, driven in part by rapidly growing public interest and positive feedback from those enthusiastic early adopter executives who thoroughly embraced Scientific Management, seems to have led them to forget or ignore how the vast majority of leaders viewed change and improvement.

Around 1925, the leaders of the Scientific Management movement began to ask themselves why more leaders did not adopt the new system given its wide-ranging benefits. They did not understand why leaders behaved this way or how to change leaders' behaviors. Nor did they understand the classification and scope of the preconceptions that command leaders' thinking and decision-making. They thought the technical and related arguments in favor of Scientific Management would be sufficient to change leaders' behaviors. After much discussion in the ensuing years, they could only guess at answers as to why leaders resisted change and improvement and did not arrive at any meaningful conclusions. Instead, they thought that the then-emerging academic discipline of social psychology would one day figure out why leaders did not do what was in their own best interest and the company's best interest. In other words, someone else would figure it out, which did indeed happen – but not by social psychologists [2-4]. Had they been able to solve the problem, they would have come up with some possible solutions to try that might have broadened the appeal of Scientific Management. *In summary, the mistake was to plow forward with a new system without understanding, in detail, how and why it might be blocked.*

5. **Presumption of Support.** Labor unions were on the ascent in America in the late 1800s and early 1900s. Taylor and his colleagues varied in their support of unions. Some viewed unions as allies in workplace improvement and necessary to create "industrial peace" between management and labor. Others were less enthusiastic about organized labor because they thought unions reduced productivity at a time of greatly increasing consumer and industrial demand – market

conditions that were favorable for both workers (employment, income) and business (sales, profits). While they did not actively campaign against unions, most thought that better management practice, better relations between management and workers, and higher wages and better training for workers would lessen the desirability or need for labor unions. Through their prior experiences, and perhaps some reasonable assumptions, Taylor and his associates believed that workers and trade union leaders would recognize these and other benefits of Scientific Management.

Scientific Management and organized labor were not in conflict with one another until 1911 when labor unrest began at the Watertown Arsenal in Watertown, Massachusetts. With engineers determining the best way to do the work, workers viewed Scientific Management as something that turned them into machines and forced them to speed up and become deskilled. Despite not encountering problems with trade unions in the two decades prior to 1911, Taylor and his associates were no doubt aware of workers' concerns. When trade union leadership finally got involved, they became vocal and long-lasting critics of Scientific Management (also referred to as "Taylorism") and subsequent forms of progressive management that impinged on workers' knowledge, skills, rights, and control over the work.

Having missed opportunities to develop important allies – independent workers and the trade unions – both Taylor and Scientific Management instead gained an enemy with increasing power and influence among politicians and the public. Had they instead been able to gain the support of independent workers and trade unions, together they would have been able to press for improvement in management thinking and practice. With sustained pressure, more business leaders might have been willing to adopt Scientific Management. *In summary, the mistake was to discount the negative sentiments that some workers had about Scientific Management and to not gain labor union leaders as allies in producing conditions that were more favorable to workers and business owners alike.*

6. **Too Focused on Production.** Because the origins of Scientific Management were in manufacturing work, the obvious application of this new system was in other companies whose main function was manufacturing. But by about 1910 (if not sooner), it was clear that Scientific Management could be applied to all work activities – accounting, general office work, purchasing [9-11], and so on, as well as to farms, churches, universities, government, and other organizations [12]. Fundamentally, the work there was as inefficient, if not more inefficient than production work.

   Yet Scientific Management's manufacturing roots were so deep, and manufacturing was such a vibrant and growing enterprise nationally and internationally, that most people did not understand or care about its applicability beyond production. And because there was so much work available for the efficiency engineers to improve manufacturing operations, less attention was paid to improving non-production work – despite this work being closely tied to production (sales and office work pace it, and thus is a major determinant of successful production). The perception that Scientific Management's greatest applicability was in manufacturing businesses proved difficult to change. *In summary, the mistake was an inability to effectively communicate the applicability of Scientific Management to all types of work.*

7. **Skepticism Over the Gains from Improvement.** One of Taylor's objectives in the development of Scientific Management was to end the constant fighting between management and workers over the surplus of productive activity – profit that accrued from sales. He wanted to devise a system of management that resulted in improved management practice, pecuniary gain for both the company and workers, and "harmonious cooperation." In his book *The Principles of Scientific Management*, Taylor emphasized the importance of cooperation [13]: "This close, intimate, personal cooperation between the management and the men is of the essence of modern scientific or task management."

   In his testimony to Congress, Taylor said in this extended passage [14]:

   > "The great revolution that takes place in the mental attitude of the two parties under scientific management is that both sides take their eyes off of the division of the surplus as

> the all-important matter, and together turn their attention toward increasing the size of the surplus until this surplus becomes so large that it is unnecessary to quarrel over how it shall be divided. They come to see that when they stop pulling against one another, and instead both turn and push shoulder to shoulder in the same direction, the size of the surplus created by their joint efforts is truly astounding. They both realize that when they substitute friendly cooperation and mutual helpfulness for antagonism and strife they are together able to make this surplus so enormously greater than it was in the past that there is ample room for a large increase in wages for the workmen and an equally great increase in profits for the manufacturer. This, gentlemen, is the beginning of the great mental revolution which constitutes the first step toward scientific management. It is along this line of complete change in the mental attitude of both sides; of the substitution of peace for war; the substitution of hearty brotherly cooperation for contention and strife; of both pulling hard in the same direction instead of pulling apart; of replacing suspicious watchfulness with mutual confidence; of becoming friends instead of enemies; it is along this line, I say, that scientific management must be developed."

Taylor saw Scientific Management as a new system

that was responsive to needs: peace, prosperity, and economic growth for employees, the company, and the nation (Figure 2-2). Thus, part of the pathway to achieving such "intimate, friendly cooperation" lay in the wages that men were paid for their work. Taylor advocated for paying workers high wages in order for the company to achieve low costs.

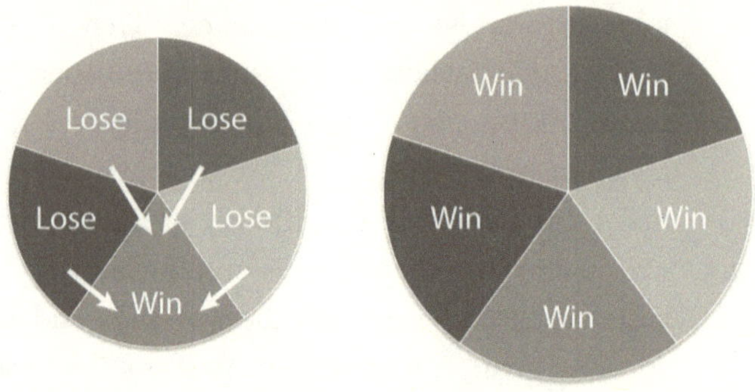

Figure 2-2. Frederick Winslow Taylor and his colleagues desired to move away from zero-sum outcomes wherein management and the company win at other stakeholders' expense, such as employees (left side). This created perpetual conflict, instead of enlarging the surplus so that everybody wins (right side); not perfectly so, but enough to satisfy.

That meant hiring and training workers to be "first-class men" – hiring fewer and better workers, training them to be more productive, and paying them more because they were better trained and more productive. Taylor had proved this concept in several companies that had adopted Scientific Management. Yet most business leaders were unable (or unwilling) to grasp how wages for workers could be high while simultaneously resulting in low costs. They perceived high wages simply as high wages, while higher productivity was understood as something they should get for free, in perpetuity. Workers, on the other hand, resisted Scientific Management because they did not believe higher wages would be forthcoming, or that higher wages would be arbitrarily cut by management – of which there were numerous real-world examples due to leaders' misunderstanding and misapplication of Scientific Management. Additionally, leaders invariably preferred to spend money on productivity-improving machine technologies versus improving work processes (see Note 8). The former was a sure thing while benefits from the latter were uncertain. Machines are an asset owned by the company and stay in place, while workers come and go; so why bother developing workers into "first-class men" and pay them more? *In summary, the mistake was to misjudge the strength and permanence of leaders' views towards workers in relation to training and higher wages.*

8. **Simple Principles, Complex Execution.** These are the five principles of Scientific Management: 1. Science, not rule of thumb. 2. Harmony, not discord. 3. Cooperation, not individualism. 4. Maximum output, in place of restricted output (see Note 9). 5. The development of each man to his greatest efficiency and prosperity. While these principles sound simple enough, it took a team of management consultants a few years to "install" Scientific Management in simple organizations and a few more years in complex organizations. This reveals a number of important things: 1) Scientific

Management is substantially different that classical management, born of preconceptions rooted in traditions. 2) Work is performed in an almost wholly non-scientific and *ad hoc* manner, both appreciated and underscored by the common managers' decree: "I don't care how you do it, just get it done." 3) Not much thought goes into work; there is far more focus on doing than thinking. 4) Leaders assume that careful thought goes into work. 5) Most organizations are in terrible shape despite being profitable. Recall what Henry Gantt said:

"The usual way of doing a thing
is always the wrong way."

To know for certain that the way of doing a thing is right or wrong cannot be based on results. It must be based on the process by which a thing is done. Therefore, one must analyze processes, and to do that one must develop methods for analyzing processes. The methods must result in the production of data, information, tables, graphs, drawings, pictures, etc., that produce objective evidence that the usual way of doing a thing is the wrong way. The development and application of these methods result from the effort of technical specialists (usually, but not exclusively, engineers) who analyze the work that people do. This is the domain of science, facts, and logical reasoning, and is where five simple principles turn into complexity. Though the five principles of Scientific Management may appeal to many business leaders, the complexity –

this new type of complexity to sort things out and improve the work – does not.

Leaders looking at financial statements see either good or bad results. How those results were achieved – in the detail of how work is performed – is inconsequential to them. They will survey their options to determine how best to make good financial results better or how to improve bad financial results. Scientific Management is one option available to them. They investigate it and find out that it requires much of them, it is complicated, it takes a long time, and a burden to them. Some will see opportunity in this, but most leaders view their numerous other options as being much more favorable. One of those more favorable options is the work of the efficiency engineers. Their willingness to improve only the parts of the business that leaders wanted (usually production), to the extent they wanted, was good enough [15]. They saw no need for an integrated system of Scientific Management either for manufacturing or for the entire company. *In summary, the mistake was to not realize the full range of options that were available to leaders, to not present to leaders the full range of options, and to show how Scientific Management was a viable contender for improving business results.*

In the roughly 40-year period between 1890 to 1930, the creators and promoters of Scientific Management had great difficulty in getting a large population of business leaders to see the need for Scientific Management. By 1915, there were several dozen examples of successful "installation" of Scientific Management [16]. And there were widely varying levels of improvement that the efficiency engineers were able to achieve in several hundred organizations using their preferred parts of Scientific Management. Overall, Scientific Management was a very important innovation in management thinking and practice that captured the attention of business leaders, government officials, academics, and the public. It was widely reported in newspapers and the trade press, and a vast literature of books and magazine articles was produced. Much of this literature circulated around the world, with key works being translated into numerous languages. Given America's prominence at the time, this American innovation was held in the highest regard by those companies seeking to become nationally and internationally competitive in trade. British, Russian, French, German, and Japanese companies, among other nationalities, carefully followed and studied the progression of Scientific Management and most other technical innovations in design and production across nearly all industries.

Yet the goal of replacing classical management, based on tradition ("rule of thumb") and preconceptions with Scientific Management based on science and sensory perceptions, largely failed. The accounting of eight principal mistakes illustrates different facets of the difficulty of achieving substantive and lasting improvement to the practice of leadership and management. When success was achieved, changes in management and changes in ownership inevitably returned leadership and management practice back to its historical norm of classical management. Nevertheless, Scientific Management led to the creation of many innovations, and in particular, the new field of industrial engineering. It laid the foundation for what was to come less than two decades later. Without Scientific Management, Toyota's production system would not have been created.

Toyota Moves Forward

When leaders of Toyoda Automatic Loom Works decided to enter automobile manufacturing in 1937 [17], top leaders seemed to realize that they could not produce vehicles the same way looms had been produced. Loom production was batch-and-queue, resulting in the accumulation of many parts, large expensive inventories, slow throughput, and a lengthy order-to-cash cycle. These increase risk and threaten survival of a new, entrepreneurial business. Like looms, automobiles contain thousands of parts. The fledgling Toyota Motor Corporation did not have the resources to produce all the necessary parts nor the facilities and manpower to manage parts inventories. So, Kiichiro Toyoda partnered with suppliers and envisioned a system of production in which the correct parts would arrive in the required number to the place they were needed at the time they were needed. He named it "just-in-time."

In addition, Kiichiro Toyoda borrowed an idea from his father's invention of the automatic power loom: *jidoka* (autonomation), or "automation with a human touch," wherein the machine stops automatically when a problem is detected [18]. This invention enabled one worker to operate several machines instead of just one machine, thus vastly increasing worker productivity. The twin ideas of just-in-time and *jidoka* went largely undeveloped due to World War II, vehicle parts shortages, and other factors. In 1943, Taiichi Ohno left Toyoda Spinning and Weaving Co. and joined Toyota Motor Corporation where he became supervisor in the engine manufacturing shop. It was there that he tried to figure out how to improve production based on Kiichiro Toyoda's idea of just-in-time and Sakichi Toyoda's invention, *jidoka.* [19]. Importantly, he and his colleagues did not assume to know the answer. All they could do to solve the problem was to experiment rapidly with different ways of doing the work. By the early 1950s, Ohno and his team of production engineers, industrial engineers, and participating workers figured out the basic outlines of how to improve production based on just-in-time and *jidoka.* They developed small lot "pull" production methods which improved the flow of material (see Note 10). This method was carried forward throughout internal manufacturing, with constant additional experimentation to further develop and improve the system, and subsequently to external suppliers to better coordinate and synchronize material and information flows.

Toyota people were just solving problems related to improving production processes and improve material and information flow by trial and error (see Note 11). There was no *a priori* blueprint or grand design to develop a new production system (see Note 12). What they created had no name for some two decades. Then, in honor of Mr. Ohno, it was named "The Ohno system." Like Frederick Winslow Taylor, Ohno-san disliked the name for similar reasons. By the early 1970s the production method that they had collaboratively developed over some 30 years was named "Toyota Production System" (TPS). Recall that in Taylor's days, most markets were sellers' markets, and so the production system, batch-and-queue was appropriate for the market condition. But, since its inception, Toyota Motor Corporation faced a competitive buyers' market, and so the development of TPS occurred under these different circumstances, resulting in a flow production system that was highly responsive to changes in customer demand – unlike the sellers' market batch-and-queue production system, ancient in its origins, and thus a characteristic part of classical management.

While the rest of the business world was working with the various remnants of Scientific Management between the late 1930s and the early 1970s, Toyota people were building upon it and created something new. Toyota's accomplishment goes largely unnoticed until a crisis struck: the 1973 oil embargo. Toyota weathered that crisis better than most other Japanese corporations or international automakers. The question was, why? Toyota leadership generously allowed outsiders (e.g. academics, reporters, consultants) to study their unique production system – not just for a year or two, but for more than four decades. They did not have to do this; Toyota Motor Corporation had no responsibility to teach TPS or their way of leadership and general management to the world. But Toyota leaders did feel that TPS could help other manufacturers and nonmanufacturers improve if they were willing to learn and help themselves, which would, in turn, result in benefits to society.

Toyota's openness resulted in the creation of an enormous body of knowledge about many different technical and non-technical aspects of TPS. Nevertheless, most researchers and others missed many important things in the first 30-plus years of study. This is easy to see in hindsight given the difficulty of Japanese-to-English interpretation and the vast tacit knowledge that underlies TPS and Toyota leaders' way of thinking. Yet, there were important clues and insights that were missed in conversations with Toyota leaders and in their writings [19, 20]. For example, in the Preface to the 1988 English edition of his 1978 book (in Japanese) Toyota Production System, Mr. Ohno said [21]:

> "The most important objective of the Toyota system has been to increase production efficiency by consistently and thoroughly eliminating waste. This concept, and the equally important respect for humanity that has passed down from the venerable Toyoda Sakichi (1867-1930), founder of the company and master of inventions, to his son Toyoda Kiichirō (1894-1952), Toyota Motor Company's first president and father of the Japanese passenger car, are the foundation of the Toyota production system."

The "equally important respect for humanity" concept connects to the work of Frederick Winslow Taylor, whose

Scientific Management system had the intention, and outcome, when "installed" correctly, to do good things for business, people, and society. This idea of respecting humans has long been foundational in progressive management (see Notes 13 and 14) because it requires the engagement of each employee to think of many ideas to improve their work. Disrespecting employees shuts down ideation, which in turn shuts down improvement, which is a fundamental objective of progressive management. In classical management, managers think and workers do, while in progressive management managers and workers think and do.

Another important clue from the Preface is this [22]:

> "The Toyota production system, however, is not just a production system. I am confident it will reveal its strength as a management system adapted to today's era of global markets and high-level computerized information systems."

Because Toyota used the name Toyota production system," those who studied it thought it was nothing more than a production system. As such, they focused on the component parts of TPS, the methods and tools (see Preface, Note 9), and most, but not all, researchers did not recognize TPS as an overall management system. Mr. Ohno said [23]:

> "Companies make a big mistake in implementing the Toyota production system thinking that it is just

> a production method. The Toyota production method won't work unless it is used as an overall management system… those who decide to implement the Toyota production system must be fully committed. If you try to adopt only the 'good parts', you'll fail."

Mr. Ohno knew from his experience with Toyota's suppliers that people are invariably drawn towards picking selected parts (tools) of the system to "implement." This recalls the earlier experience of Scientific Management in which there was far more interest in its parts than the entire system. Former Toyota president Fujio Cho had this to say about Toyota's management system after researchers and others had studied and written about it for more than 30 years [24]:

> "Our way of thinking is very difficult to copy or even to understand."

It seems he understood that people outside of Toyota had not really grasped the essence of TPS and the Toyota Way.

Another former Toyota president, Katsuaki Watanabe said this about the difficulty that even insiders have in understanding the Toyota Way [25]:

> "There's no end to the process of learning about the Toyota Way. I don't think I have a complete understanding even today, and I have worked for the company for 43 years."

These quotes point to two important things: 1) the complexity of the system and 2) its unknowability. Even though the basic principles, "continuous improvement" and "respect for people" are simple, their realization in practice (application to problem-solving, particularly simplification) can be complex in relation to the sustained practice necessary to understand and master the basics. The difficulty in knowing TPS and the Toyota Way results from a management system that continuously evolves in response to changing conditions internally within the company and externally in the marketplace. This contrasts with Scientific Management, where the system was more or less fixed in Taylor's understanding, practice, and advocacy of it, though Henry Gantt and Frank and Lillian Gilbreth saw Scientific Management as needing to possess more evolutionary characteristics. Toyota's progressive management system also contrasts with classical management in that the latter is easily knowable [2-4, Appendix I] – and knowing (or the appearance of knowing) is a *required* leadership trait. Hence the ubiquity of classical management.

Part of the unknowability of TPS and the Toyota Way is due to the application of human ideation and creativity in problem-solving – especially when nearly all employees are engaged in such activity. The system evolves on its own based on certain broad guidelines such as founding principles and guiding principles (See Appendix I). An important problem-solving method is kaizen. This method utilizes people's ideas and creativity to solve problems at low cost or no cost, and cumulatively gain the learning and wisdom necessary to solve future problems. The following quotes from Toyota leaders emphasize the importance of kaizen [26-28]:

> "The philosophy that makes [kaizen] possible is 'Respect for People'." – Fujio Cho

> "…kaizen, or continuous improvement. You never reach a final stage. The key is making tomorrow better than today. After the kaizen is also before the kaizen; when one improvement is finished, it is the beginning of the next improvement." – Akio Toyoda

> "…we at Toyota are people 'who believe there is always a better way.' Every kaizen improvement is the beginning of other kaizen improvements. Kaizen is an unending process. All of us at Toyota share a commitment to that fundamental principle of the Toyota Way." – Akio Toyoda

A long-term commitment by Toyota managers to allow people to think, ascertain the facts via kaizen and other unique derivative problem-solving methods, and make improvements rapidly enabled the creative development and continuing evolution of TPS and the Toyota Way (see Note 15). Nothing like this can be achieved under the aegis of classical management. The learning from the past for classical management is that it is a workable though imperfect system that needs only occasional minor adjustment. The learning from the past for progressive management is that it too is a workable though imperfect system in need of never-ending daily continuous improvement (see Note 16).

Toyota people moved forward methodically and meticulously with Scientific Management and industrial engineering to improve production. They built upon the work of others before them. They contributed their own unique way of thinking. They borrowed ideas and methods, and they invented ideas and methods. And they ended up creating something new: a more advanced coherent and integrated system of corporate management. They created a *new management technology*, where "technology" is understood in its common form as "the application of scientific knowledge for practical purposes" – with the management of organizations being one such practical purpose (see Note 17). This remarkable achievement, still undergoing evolution, remains poorly understood and extraordinarily underappreciated by business leaders, academics (e.g. business, management, economics, psychology, sociology, and engineering professors), politicians, workers, unions, and the public.

However, researchers from various disciplines, and certain other interested persons, did appreciate what Toyota accomplished, to the varying extent of their abilities to understand it. The result of all the research was to make much of Toyota's proprietary management system public and to make it available to others in simplified and generic forms which may or may not produce the desired outcome of material and information flow based on just-in-time and *jidoka*. In the years since 1973, countless numbers have tried to turn Toyota's management system, in whole or part, into a commercial product and service. If one does this, they should do so carefully because the simplicity of the principles ("continuous improvement" and "respect for people") and concepts such as eliminating waste deceive people into thinking they know more than they do given the complexity of the system and its unknowability. These being the facts, they have a serious responsibility to get it as right as they can as soon as they can, on a continuing basis, because people will take that information, knowledge, or training and put it into practice in live business settings. In doing so, the enthusiastic adopters of simplified and generic forms of Toyota's management system could make many significant errors, such as impair quality or delivery, increase costs, create ergonomic problems, loss of employment, or cause professional harm to themselves when things don't go as planned. In other words, mistakes in understanding and presenting simplified and generic forms of Toyota's management system to business leaders and the employees who do the work of "implementation" will have negative consequences all around. The next section identifies the principal mistakes made in the formulation and advancement of the current premier formulation of progressive management, Lean management.

Lean Management Mistakes

A large academic study of the automobile industry and Toyota Motor Corporation's production system in the 1980s [29] led to the creation of what became known as "lean production." The term "lean" came into the business realm in a paper published in *Sloan Management Review* in the fall of 1988 [30]. The word "lean" was undefined in the paper and presumably intended to be both a synonym and a generic term for Toyota's production system, so named "because it uses less of everything compared with mass production" [31]. While at the time the paper was published manufacturing was headed into decline in the United States, the paper and a subsequent more detailed work [30] were seen by some business leaders as a pathway for strengthening manufacturing and assuring its survival. This led to follow-on work by the principal investigators which extended and elaborated the concepts and defined five principles of "lean" [32]. These works proved to be very influential and generated great interest in "lean production."

The popularity of these works led to the formation of a widely dispersed "lean movement" – specific persons identifiable as thought leaders and followers worldwide who subscribed to the Lean ideology. It spawned conferences, scores of trade books and articles, and extensive academic research. While the movement began first with businesses whose primarily function is manufactured goods, it later spread to service businesses, non-profit organizations, and government. The Lean movement has grown steadily since its inception (see Note 18) based on its conceptual simplicity and the apparent relative ease of use of selected methods and tools that originated with Toyota.

Table 1 compares a 1983 description of Toyota Production System written by Yasuhiro Monden [33] to the 2020 description of Lean from the Lean Enterprise Institute, the

Table 1. Descriptions of TPS and Lean

TPS (1983)	Lean (2020)
"...although cost-reduction is the system's most important goal, it must achieve three other subgoals in order to achieve its primary objective. They include: 1. Quantity control, which enables the system to adapt to daily and monthly fluctuations in demand in terms of quantities and variety; 2. Quality assurance, which assures that each process will supply only good units to subsequent processes; 3. Respect-for-humanity, which must be cultivated while the system utilizes the human resources to obtain its cost objectives. It should be emphasized here that these three goals cannot exist independently or be achieved independently without influencing each other or the primary goal of cost reduction. It is a special feature of the Toyota production system that the primary goal cannot be achieved without realization of the subgoals and vice versa. All goals are outputs of the same system; with productivity as the ultimate purpose and guiding concept, the Toyota production system strives to realize each of the goals for which it has been designed."	"The core idea is to maximize **customer value** while minimizing waste. Simply, lean means creating more value for customers with fewer resources. A lean organization understands customer value and focuses its key processes to continuously increase it. The ultimate goal is to provide perfect value to the customer through a perfect value creation process that has zero waste. To accomplish this, lean thinking changes the focus of management from optimizing separate technologies, assets, and vertical departments to optimizing the flow of products and services through entire value streams that flow horizontally across technologies, assets, and departments to customers. Eliminating waste along entire value streams, instead of at isolated points, creates processes that need less human effort, less space, less capital, and less time to make products and services at far less costs and with much fewer defects, compared with traditional business systems. Companies are able to respond to changing customer desires with high variety, high quality, low cost, and with very fast throughput times. Also, information management becomes much simpler and more accurate."
Source: [33]	Source: [34]. Bold text in original.

self-described "global leader in lean management thinking, practice, and innovation" [34]. The 1983 description of TPS remains accurate today, though Toyota's management system was more fully characterized in 2001 in a 13-page internal document called "The Toyota Way 2001" [35]. This document "expresses the beliefs and values shared by all of us" and lacks a concise definition of the management system. A 1992 booklet titled "The Toyota Production System" provided a useful and concise definition of the management system [36]:

> "…[development of] systems and equipment that encourage employees to take the initiative in identifying and implementing better ways of doing things."

A 1998 revision of the booklet provided this definition [37]:

> "The Toyota Production System is a framework for conserving resources by eliminating waste. People who participate in the system learn to identify expenditures of material, effort, and time that do not generate value for customers. In other words, they learn to recognize waste. They also learn to take the initiative in developing measures for eliminating waste and preventing its recurrence."

It went on to say:

> "…is a reminder that lasting gains in productivity and quality are possible whenever and wherever

> management and employees are united in a commitment to positive change"

A comparison of these two definitions and Table 1 immediately reveals some similarities as well as substantial differences between Toyota's management system and Lean. This is not completely unexpected because Lean management is a "Western" interpretation of Toyota's management system. It is impossible for Lean management to be a high-fidelity representation of Toyota management due to language, culture, preconceptions, and other barriers. The significant point is that the two are not the same, even though they share a common source (see Note 19). If understood and practiced correctly, both can produce favorable, albeit different, results. Additionally, organizations uptake Lean management and alter it in ways deemed necessary to make it one's own. As a result, there exists many flavors of Lean management, peculiar to local understanding of Lean principles and practices, limitations imposed by managers, and the needs of the business. Lean can exist in forms ranging from weak to strong, the former producing little or no business results while the latter being closer to Toyota and producing a wide range of favorable business results (see Note 20).

The bringing forth of Lean production (later, Lean management) to the community of business consumers from its Toyota source is fraught with difficulties and the likelihood of many mistakes – in much the same ways as Scientific Management. But because that history was deemed irrelevant, or because of other priorities, mistakes were repeated. The following pages present the principal mistakes that have been made in the past or continue to be made. These mistakes take two forms: mistakes repeated from the days of Scientific Management and mistakes that are unique to Lean management.

The previous recounting of Scientific Management mistakes is summarized as follows:

1. **Giving the System a Name.** *The mistake was to give it a name.*

2. **Making Ineffective Arguments.** *The mistake was to focus on technical, and later, economic arguments, because neither produced the desired results of abandoning classical management nor improving efficiency.*

3. **Dramatizing the Magnitude of Change.** *The mistake was to characterize the change in management thinking and practice as something grandiose, immense, and lofty.*

4. **Not Understanding How Leaders Think.** *The mistake was to plow forward with a new system without understanding, in detail, how and why it might be blocked.*

5. **Presumption of Support.** *The mistake was to discount the negative sentiments that some workers had about Scientific Management and to not gain labor union leaders as allies in producing conditions that were more favorable to workers and business owners alike.*

6. **Too Focused on Production.** *The mistake was an inability to effectively communicate the applicability of Scientific Management to all types of work.*

7. **Skepticism Over the Gains from Improvement.** *The mistake was to misjudge the strength and permanence of leaders' views towards workers in relation to training and higher wages.*

8. **Simple Principles, Complex Execution.** *The mistake was to not realize the full range of options that were available to leaders, to not present to leaders the full range of options, and to show how Scientific Management was a viable contender for improving business results.*

Not surprisingly, Lean management suffered these same eight mistakes:

1. Like Scientific Management before it, it had to have a name. While seemingly sensible at the time, giving progressive management a name creates additional opportunities for criticism and repudiation. Many other names have been suggested but none are likely to be much better. "Lean" has gained a pejorative connotation as being associated with layoffs and other bad outcomes for employees as well as the company (see Chapter 2). It is unlikely that this can be corrected.

2. Like Scientific Management before it, Lean made ineffective arguments for its adoption. It began with technical arguments and quickly evolved into economic arguments. People have moved past these and will try

any argument they can think of. Like Scientific Management before it, arguments are persuasive to only a very small number of business leaders.

3. Like Scientific Management before it, Lean management was characterized as something grandiose, immense, and lofty – "Lean transformation." Leaders must change from "traditional thinking" to "Lean thinking." In his book *Toyota Production System*, Taiichi Ohno called for a "revolution in consciousness" and a "revolution in thinking" [38]. Lean devotees also spoke of a "Lean revolution,' "revolution in thinking" "revolutionizing manufacturing," "revolutionizing healthcare," and so on. Business leaders do not like that kind of talk. It conjures an idealism that pragmatists detest and a disturbance they will do everything to avoid.

4. Like Scientific Management before it, Lean promoters and practitioners did not understand how top managers think, and still do not [2-4, Appendix I]. They keep trying the same things to gain leaders' support and hope to achieve a different result. They did not understand how and why Lean transformation would be blocked. Lean transformation success remains a rare occurrence. And like Scientific Management before it, they thought it would be relatively easy to change leader's behaviors and did not understand the classification and scope of the preconceptions that command leaders' thinking and decision-making.

5. Like Scientific Management before it, they did not gain the support of labor unions and non-union workers. There was (and still is) no pull for Lean management from workers. The focus was on top leaders and creating an army of salaried professional staff to convince leaders to abandon classical management.

6. Like Scientific Management before it, Lean was too focused on production for too many years. The change in name from "lean production" to "Lean management" occurred in 2007 (see Note 21), nearly 20 years after the term "lean" came into the business realm. This cemented the general understanding of Lean as a "manufacturing thing," which remains to this day despite numerous examples of Lean principles and practices applied to service, non-profits, and other types of organizations.

7. Like Scientific Management before it, most workers did not realize additional remuneration as a result of cost reduction and productivity and quality improvement. Few organizations had quarterly profit-sharing or instituted profit-sharing, which is known to help facilitate Lean transformations. Curiously, and speaking in general terms, neither shop floor workers, office workers, nor salaried staff expected or demanded higher pay as a result of their efforts to apply Lean principles and practices.

8. Like Scientific Management before it, Lean has simple principles but its execution is complicated – though

less so than either Scientific Management or Toyota Management. They too did not realize the range of options other than Lean that are available to top leaders to improve business performance. For most leaders, Lean is the last choice among many.

Plus ça change, plus c'est la même chose; the more things change, the more they stay the same. Not exactly so, but, in this case, pretty close. People also commonly say "the past is the past; it's time to move on." Indeed. So, moving on into the future hopefully means to not repeat these eight mistakes when the next major version of progressive management comes along. It also means to not repeat the following six mistakes that are unique to the development and advancement of Lean.

9. **Did Not Engage the Public.** The community of people interested in Lean management speak mostly to themselves. There is no person or organization whose focused role is to inform the general public about Lean management. While there are many websites dedicated to disseminating information about Lean management, they are almost exclusively for the existing Lean audience. Most of these websites are very good, as are many blogs, videos, and other information resources.

   A few times a year there are stories about Lean management or some aspect of it in influential business periodicals such as *The Wall Street Journal*, *Financial Times*, *The New York Times*, and the like. Generally, such articles contain significant inaccuracies, mistakes, and misrepresentations that tend do more harm to Lean management than good. There is no person or organizations assigned to correct the facts. Additionally, the understanding of Lean management even among its followers is wide-ranging, from accurate to the absurd. Therefore, the likelihood of confusing the public is great. Scientific Management was more successful at engaging the public perhaps because it was easier for laypersons to understand. It is not clear that efforts have been made to make Lean management easy to understand for consumption by laypersons (e.g. as in a print advertisement or a 10- or 30-second commercial). *In summary, the mistake was to not devote resources to educating the general public about Lean management.*

10. **Belated recognition of "Respect for Humanity."** "Cooperation" [5, 6], "Respect for Humanity" "Respect for People" [20, 35], "Benefit for All [39], or similar concept is part of the history of progressive management for more than 120 years. It is required for progressive management to function correctly and produce continuous positive change. Without this principle, employees will not engage in improvement. Without this principle they fear being harmed and will do nothing more than produce the appearance of improvement. So, there must exist a principle that all employees, including managers, abide by to make progressive management work, and not focus solely on the technical aspect of continuous improvement.

    Unfortunately, Lean management did not recognize this

principle until late 2007 [40] and early 2008 [41], more than six years after The Toyota Way 2001 document was published and making "Respect for People" explicit – consistent with the prior history of progressive management going back more than 100 years. When "Respect for People" was recognized, it was limited to the manager-worker dyad, not the full complement of primary stakeholders as intended: employees, suppliers, customers, investors, and communities [42]. The leaders of the Lean movement, having had access to Toyota senior managers for some two decades prior, appear to have missed this important aspect of Toyota's management system. For some 20 years post-1988, when "lean production" came into the business realm, the focus among Lean movement leaders, other Lean promoters and practitioners, and business leaders was "continuous improvement," not both "continuous improvement" and "respect for people." Consequently, to business leaders, Lean management looked like a good way to reduce costs by laying people off after improvements in productivity had been achieved. And that, along with globalization, cost a lot of people their jobs. There is little documentary evidence that Lean movement leaders tried to correct business leaders' misunderstanding and misapplication of Lean management before or after 2007 (see Note 22).

The harm caused by layoffs attributed to Lean, with causality being sometimes fair and other times unfair, likely poisoned some portion of Generation X, Millennials, and perhaps Generation Z to the idea of progressive Lean management. While these younger generations appear to demand better business leadership and management of organizations, they typically do not turn to Lean management as a solution. *In summary, the mistake was to not focus on "respect for people" from the start, positioning it as a requirement in order to engage employees in continuous improvement.*

11. **Lean Tools over Mindset.** The general approach taken was to train people how to use Lean tools and to practice using the tools, and from that they would learn the mindset of continuous improvement. Evidence of this is the proliferation of books focused on Lean tools such as value stream mapping, A3 reports, gemba walks, kata, coaching, leader standard work, strategy deployment, product development, etc. Though the content of these books may be put it into the larger context of Lean management, they invariably are used in isolation of one another (see Preface, Note 8). Some of this reductionism from system to tools is promulgated by business leaders who have no need for a new system of management but do perceive a need for new tools that can help workers solve problems. Workers dutifully take up the tools. Some use them correctly while most others use them incorrectly. Either way, compliance is assured. Managers, seeing evidence of the use of new Lean tools is satisfied, but soon they wonder why little improvement has been achieved.

Toshihiro Nagamatsu, former CEO Shingijutsu USA, explains the mindset of improvement this way [43]:

> "We are always at our worst. You may think you are a good company today, but make no mistake you are not. You may become better tomorrow, but still you are toward the back. At any moment, somewhere in this world there is someone doing the same work better. There is no end. You must continually seek to improve."

Unlike Mr. Nagamatsu's harsh, perhaps even insulting characterization learned from his work at Toyota, the Lean mindset about improvement is soft; more along the lines of "oh, just do the best you can." If someone does a little bit better than they have done in the past, then that easily qualifies as having done the best they can. That mindset does not challenge people to do *a lot better* than they have ever done before. It does not challenge them to confront their preconceptions and destroy them. In the book *Just-In-Time For Today and Tomorrow*, Taiichi Ohno said [44]:

> "We are doomed to failure without a daily destruction of our various preconceptions."

That means failure on a personal level as well as failure to creatively develop a better system of management. This must be the mindset of improvement for managers and workers alike; to go beyond one's self-imposed limitations or the limitations imposed by one's peers or the institution of leadership. It is rare for this to occur on its own; it is usually cultivated through the guidance of one who has gone before and experienced such transcendence. *In summary, the mistake was to focus on Lean tools instead of focusing on the mindset of improvement.*

12. **Betting it All on Leadership Behaviors.** The study of modern business leadership began in earnest in the mid-1920s [45, 46]. The focus then, as now, was on leadership behaviors. There is an unstoppable train of thought that changing leadership behaviors is the answer to the problem of why leaders resist or reject Lean management. The continuing hope that this is the solution is magical thinking. Nearly 100 years of good research on leadership behaviors and books by leaders on their secrets of success have yielded little results [47-49]. While it is a captivating and mesmerizing topic, it is largely a path to nowhere. Nevertheless, Lean devotees continue, almost uniformly, to believe this is the one smartest path forward, all the while complaining about the business leaders that don't "get it" and glorifying those few business leaders that do "get it." Despite their presumed problem-solving prowess, Lean movement leaders and Lean practitioners clearly see leadership behaviors as the problem when it is only a surface-level manifestation of deeper problems. There is no desire to dig deeper perhaps because they fear what they will find.

    What they will find is a problem that is much more complicated, confusing, distasteful, and disturbing than they imagine [2-4, Appendix I], and that easy solutions are unlikely to exist. Avoidance of the facts conveniently keeps hopes alive and the army of Lean people devoted to the cause. But there is a cost to this. It deposes Lean management from a position of objective superiority to luck. Meaning, business leaders who embrace Lean management are the result of luck rather than by the design of alluring factual arguments or seductive salesmanship declaring the superiority of Lean management over classical management. There is an unusual stubbornness here that undercuts deep inquiry (asking "why?") and continuous learning; an inability to destroy one's preconceptions related to leaders and leadership behaviors. *In summary, the mistake was to remain stuck on leadership behaviors as the solution for recruiting new Lean leaders.*

13. **Time Function of Improvement.** The Lean management literature is full of useful information about the technical and behavioral aspects of improvement. But one thing is almost always missing: How long does improvement take? How long should improvement take? We know that like Scientific Management, Lean transformation takes years to "implement." But what happens during those years, months, weeks, days, and hours that eventually result in transformation? The time function of improvement is missing. Absent this information, people will assume that improvement in the context of Lean management should take about as long as it does outside of that context – a long time, as it is in the world of classical management where change proceeds very slowly.

Improvement in the context of Lean management should be rapid – hours or a few days, or perhaps a week or two. But mostly it should be hours or a few days. And a lot should be accomplished during that time by the individual or team assigned to make improvements. Yet most organizations make improvements not only slowly, but they slow it down further by atomizing improvement work into its component parts. It is common for teams to spend several days on 5S or to create a value stream map, when these are activities that should be completed in hours. This work, often facilitated by consultants, generates huge billable hours but miniscule business results. People lose interest, energy, and enthusiasm when improvement takes a long time. Things that take a long time are usually unpleasant. People are busy and they will find other things to do. When the pace of improvement is slow, the accumulation of business results is slow and then leaders become agitated. When leaders are agitated, they get more involved and more micromanaging of improvement activities that they know little about. The result is employees shift their focus to producing the appearance of improvement. This is not what should be happening. It is a failure to understand the essence of improvement.

The point of pushing people to improve rapidly is to

- Improve teamwork
- Challenge individuals and teams
- Focus people's attention
- Generate curiosity and interest

- Compel them to think differently about the nature of problems and possible solutions
- Apply human creative and innovative capabilities
- Destroy their preconceptions
- Generate enthusiasm for experimentation and problem-solving

When these things happen, people achieve things they never thought possible. They feel energized about the process of improvement and what they accomplished and they had fun and want to do it again and again. They will take the initiative to improve when future problems arise. The experience of improvement must be such that cycle time from initial engagement to final result – the reward for having accomplished something challenging – is quick. It must happen, usually, in hours or days. This is the most important thing that has been missing from the Lean literature (and Toyota literature as well). *In summary, the mistake was to not elaborate on the time function and spirit of improvement.*

14. **Human Creativity in Improvement.** Toyota's production system came into being mostly through massive amounts of trial and error. In contrast to controlled scientific experiments, trial and error is quasi-systematic and more characteristic of an engineering approach to problem-solving. Realization of a problem leads to varied attempts to solve it, and the solution either solves the problem, in which case efforts continue to make further improvements, or the solution worked but it created new problems to solve. Since there was no

recipe or book to follow, Toyota people had to think and generate ideas. The unique thing was that they had to do so within a basic framework of thinking that a) conditions were dire, b) survival was at stake, and c) resources, particularly money, were not available. The solutions they came up with were imaginative if not ingenious. Such human creativity inspired others and instilled confidence to adapt and do the impossible, and, importantly, resulted in remarkable business success. This basic framework of thinking exists in Toyota today, and management views it (and kaizen) as vital to future success. Most businesses do not operate based on all three elements of the framework: conditions are dire, survival is perpetually at stake, and resources, particularly money, are not available. Consequently, creativity in problem-solving is generally much less than human potential. Often it is more akin to rote problem-solving with little additional effort to further improve. People do not realize the extent to which one must "struggle to squeeze your intelligence out." Overall, the Lean literature has not sufficiently emphasized the basic framework for creativity in problem-solving and the level of imagination and creativity that is required. *In summary, the mistake was to not elaborate on the conditions, nature, and extent of human creativity required for improvement.*

Here is a summary of the 14 principal Lean management mistakes (see Note 23):

1. **Giving the System a Name.** *The mistake was to give it a name.*

2. **Making Ineffective Arguments.** *The mistake was focus on technical, and later, economic arguments, because neither produced the desired results of abandoning classical management nor improving efficiency.*

3. **Dramatizing the Magnitude of Change.** *The mistake was to characterize the change in management thinking and practice as something grandiose, immense, and lofty.*

4. **Not Understanding How Leaders Think.** *The mistake was to plow forward with a new system without understanding, in detail, how and why it might be blocked.*

5. **Presumption of Support.** *The mistake was to discount the negative sentiments that some workers had about Lean management and to not gain labor union leaders as allies in producing conditions that were more favorable to workers and business owners alike.*

6. **Too Focused on Production.** *The mistake was an inability to effectively communicate the applicability of Lean management to all types of work.*

7. **Skepticism Over the Gains from Improvement.** *The mistake was to misjudge the strength and permanence of leaders' views towards workers in relation to training and higher wages.*

8. **Simple Principles, Complicated Execution.** *The mistake was to not realize the full range of options that were available to leaders, to not present to leaders the full range of options, and to show how Lean management was a viable*

contender for improving business results.

9. **Did Not Engage the Public.** *In summary, the mistake was to not devote resources to educating the general public about Lean management.*

10. **Belated recognition of "Respect for Humanity."** *In summary, the mistake was to not focus on "respect for people" from the start, positioning it as a requirement in order to engage employees in continuous improvement.*

11. **Lean Tools over Mindset.** *In summary, the mistake was to focus on Lean tools instead of focusing on the mindset of improvement.*

12. **Betting it All on Leadership Behaviors.** *In summary, the mistake was to remain stuck on leadership behaviors as the solution for recruiting new Lean leaders.*

13. **Time Function of Improvement.** *In summary, the mistake was to not elaborate on the time function and spirit of improvement.*

14. **Human Creativity in Improvement.** *In summary, the mistake was to not elaborate on the conditions, nature, and extent of human creativity required for improvement.*

There are other mistakes, most of which are less significant but nonetheless important in relation to the successful advancement of human-centered progressive management. Additional mistakes can be found in the extant literature.

As this Chapter has shown, the past is a fruitful source for learning especially for those who seek positive change by breaking the status quo. In a paper from 1911 titled "The Spirit in Which Scientific Management Should be Approached" [50], James Mapes Dodge, Chairman of the Board of The Link-Belt Company in Philadelphia, Pennsylvania, had this to say about leaders' spirit, or lack thereof, for Scientific Management – with the same being true today about leaders and Lean management, as well as anyone in the future who is interested in progressive management:

> "Probably with all of us it is more difficult to accept a modification of a belief than to absorb a most startling or revolutionary new idea which does not call for any reversal of a notion to which we have tenaciously held. So in this matter of management it was, and is, and always will be essential for us to keep a hopeful equilibrium during transition from our old to our new love; and this transition period is certain to be a trying one. In the establishments with which I am connected conversion came slowly to nearly all, and some of those who, it would seem, should logically have accepted the innovation with avidity, seemed temperamentally incapable of such acceptance. Those who live entirely in the present, without thought of the future or of the past, can easily acquire the habit of doing things in a new way; but those having active minds are apt to waver between the necessity of advancing a decision and the fear of error born of caution and imagination.

> Even a measure of intelligence might show that an ardent accepter of Scientific Management and a man unalterably opposed to it in every form, are of the same brain capacity. There is temperamental sectarianism in every profession and walk of life, inexplicable because temperament is inexplicable."

"Thought of the future or of the past" – one's preconceptions about what has been and what should be – prevents progress, the "transition from our old to our new love."

Paraphrasing the final sentence of Mr. Dodge's paper, he said:

> Everlasting ignorance is to condemn
> before investigating.

These words highlight the ever-present danger to the advancement of progressive management and to progressive management itself, for those who subscribe to progressive management can fall prey to the human habit of "temperamental sectarianism" – inexplicable then, but not so now.

Notes

1. More apt descriptions for the intellectual heritage of classical management would be "imbecile" or "ignoramus." The former meaning stupid in the sense of avoidance of the facts leads to problems that are much bigger than the facts themselves (e.g. Boeing 737 Max crashes, Wells Fargo fraud, opioid drugmakers and distributors, etc.), while the latter meaning is in the sense of willful ignorance or avoidance of the facts, particularly those that could alter decision-making, resource allocation, power, rights, and privileges. Thorstein Veblen regarded as "imbecile" any institution, including the institution of leadership, as that which prevents a community of people from making progress through problem-solving: "…history records more frequent and more spectacular instances of the triumph of imbecile institutions over life and culture than of peoples who have by force of instinctive insight saved themselves alive out of a desperately precarious institutional situation…" (*Instinct of Workmanship*, 1914, p. 25).

2. In the context of engineering and science, there is no special regard for instinct as there is with leadership because it is understood through empiricism to be less useful and less reliable than the facts. The atavistic relic that remains with engineers and scientists is "serendipity," commonly known as "luck." However, careful study often reveals the existence of a clear path (process) to discovery that the discoverer does not recognize. Hence, serendipity.

3. Some of the difficulty stems from the ability of those in support of classical management or progressive management to make strong analytical and experiential arguments that justify the correctness of each. The two groups see the same problem, effective management of people and organizations, differently. Both are more or less immune to the others' well-reasoned arguments, each seeing the other as a failure and threat to one another's survival. The catalyst necessary to break the logjam has yet to appear.

4. It is difficult to determine if the desire to ignore and move on is the result of self-interest driven by the forces, singularly or combined, of pecuniary gain, ignorance, indolence, stubbornness, and delusion.

5. The name "progressive management" is also problematic due to confusion between how it is defined in this book (see p. vi) and the use of the word "progressive" in politics which often carries a negative connotation. In its day, Scientific Management greatly influenced the thinking of social and political progressive leaders, and some of its ideas were turned into policy at the federal level of government – and much reviled by those affiliated with social and political conservatism. Because politics generally has a bias in favor of maintaining the status quo, progressivism is usually disparaged – so much so that one is expected to quietly accept the status quo and also be sympathetic to their annoyance and discomfort with ideas and desires for change and improvement. If the term "progressive management" is carried forward, then there will likely be a need for focused and long-term effort to inform the public of the

difference in meaning.

6. Taylor and his team thought poorly of efficiency engineers whose main purpose was to enrich themselves at the expense of workers who were often laid off after gains in efficiency had been achieved. The efficiency engineers thought poorly of Taylor and his team for their inability to compromise their principles and adjust their practices to deliver the service that business leaders wanted. It should be no surprise that the efficiency engineers (referred disparagingly as "fakirs, quacks, cranks, and charlatans") were far more financially successful as management consultants than Taylor and his team. Business leaders were then, as now, gullible to the efficiency engineer's sales pitch for quick fixes. Taylor said, correctly, "The writer has over and over again warned those who contemplated making this change that it was a matter, even in a simple establishment, of from two to three years, and that in some cases it requires from four to five years" [6].

7. An exception was Frank Gilbreth, who with the influence of his wife, industrial psychologist Lillian Gilbreth, were a bit more flexible in their practice of Scientific Management (see L.M. Gilbreth (1914), *The Psychology of Management*, Sturgis and Walton Co., New York, New York), as was Henry Gantt, also likely influenced by the thinking and writing of Lillian Gilbreth. By 1914 or 1915, both the Gilbreths and Gantt realized that the idea of continuous improvement, with input from operators, was a better path to pursue than solely engineers searching to find "the one best way" for operators to do the job.

8. Referring to Figure 2-2, the introduction of machine technology in the workplace almost always has the effect of creating win-lose situations. Therefore, a competition exists between that and efforts to create non-zero-sum outcomes via progressive management. Those skilled in progressive management seek to assure that machine technology is truly needed and that any harm that is caused to people is ameliorated. The change in the distribution of surplus caused by the introduction of machine technology is highly sought after in classical management because it accrues favorably to the interests of owners.

9. At that time in America, most markets were sellers' markets, so sellers could easily sell everything they made. Markets generally shifted to buyers' markets after World War II. That required a new management system, reflected in the creative development of Toyota's management system whose roots are Scientific Management.

10. Batch-and-queue is a method of producing goods where materials are processed in large batches, which results in long queue times between operations. While this term originated in manufacturing, the conventional method for delivering services is also batch-and-queue (i.e. processing information in large batches). Batch-and-queue processing results in lower quality and higher cost products or services. In contrast flow production is achieved by processing material or information in small lots, lots as small as single piece, to achieve a continuous flow whose rate of production is paced by the rate of customer demand. A flow production system avoids overproduction (high inventory

costs, discounting) and underproduction (lost sales) that plagues batch-and-queue material and information processing.

11. In his book, *Toyota Production System*, Mr. Ohno used the term "rationalization" to describe the unique form of rapid trial and error experimentation that Toyota developed: kaizen.

12. Toyota people vigorously pursued the dialectic between exogenous (market; customer and competitor) factors and endogenous factors (from within, based on needs). Lots of kaizen (rapid trial and error experimentation) to fit production processes to the buyers' market.

13. "Respect for Humanity" and "Respect for People" defy simple definition. Anyone who has a lot of experience with progressive management knows that a simple definition cannot fully capture the meaning. Defining "Respect for Humanity" or "Respect for People" will fool people into thinking they know what it means. They will become lazy and avoid thinking for themselves. A definition puts limits on one's ability to grow their understanding over time, closing off hundreds, if not thousands of different ways to understand this concept. It is comprehended through daily practice, on the job, and in combination with kaizen. It can never be completely comprehended.

14. See Woollard, F. G. and Emiliani, B. (2009), *Principles of Mass and Flow Production*, 55th Anniversary Special Reprint Edition, The CLBM, LLC, Wethersfield, Connecticut.

(original date of publication of *Principles of Mass and Flow Production* was 1954).

15. In this quote, Mr. Fujio Cho, who reported directly to Taiichi Ohno, provides a more complete description of kaizen and how it functions within Toyota: "The corporate culture of Toyota is characterized by an endless pursuit of innovation. We use the word 'kaizen,' or continuous improvement, which has received much attention over the years at home and abroad. It is the first word that comes to mind when we think of Toyota. Promoting innovation through kaizen means keeping abreast with changing times through a daily and repetitive process of constant trial and error efforts that lead to tangible and effective improvements, which are then spread horizontally across the company. Kaizen is therefore constant change, or a daily commitment to improvement on a daily, incremental basis. In order for kaizen to work, it must be driven by needs and goals so that people will be motivated to achieve them. Education and training of your people is therefore vital... and people must be allowed to think." Source: "Our Endless Challenge Toward Innovation," speech by Mr. Fujio Cho, President, Toyota Motor Corporation, *Nikkei Global Management Forum*, Tokyo, Japan, 21 October 2003.

16. In an interview a few weeks later, Mr. Fujio Cho comments on the importance of the system and its daily improvement via kaizen: "Many good companies try to practice kaizen and use various TPS tools. But what is important is having all the elements together as a system. It must be practiced every day in a consistent manner – not in

spurts – in a concrete way…If I am asked to cite only one thing that makes Toyota different from other firms, it is this: everybody understands there will be no end to 'kaizen' efforts." Source: Source: Mr. Fujio Cho, President, Toyota Motor Corporation, in "Toyota's Ideals (7): Getting Firm's Work Philosophy to Help Society," *The Nikkei Weekly*, 12 November 2003.

17. In pages 69-71 of his book *Toyota Production System*, Mr. Ohno describes *ninjutsu* ("the art of invisibility") and *gijutsu* (technology); how the management practice of a technologist centers upon taking quick action, the result of extensive training based on facts. This contrasts with "management magic" – management by arithmetic, a pejorative characterization of the non-scientific status of classical management. One might think that it would be a minor, almost trivial, inconvenience for leaders to abandon management magic and instead learn to manage as Ohno-san describes, *ninjutsu* coupled with *gijutsu* – management skills learned through creative and innovative training on-the-job (i.e. kaizen) versus classroom training [51]. After all, the new management technology is merely an evolution in management practice that changing times dictate. But a preference for statis [2-4] leaves one technologically behind the times, in contrast to TPS and the Toyota Way which requires being alert to problems and taking action quickly. Unfortunately, it is common to see people educated in science and engineering and who worked for years in those fact-based disciplines embodying careful observation and skepticism, get promoted to executive levels and succumb to "management magic." Their education and work

experience as technologists do not typically result in progressive change as one would hope or expect. Instead, they are engulfed by the institution of leadership and its demand that all members do their part to maintain the status quo, *de jure*. This shows that the ethos of engineering and science can be easily reversed. Therein lies an opportunity for improvement.

18. There is some evidence that as of 2020, there is a slower rate of growth of the Lean movement, possibly a leveling off or even a decline. The equivocation is the result of the popularity of Lean simultaneously increasing and decreasing in various regions globally. For example, the Lean movement currently appears to be in decline in the United States but increasing rapidly in Latin America. There is a general view that Lean, to varying extents, has been incorporated into management practice, which would account for a slower rate of growth (or leveling off or decline). Lean borrows heavily from methods and tools developed by Toyota. While these tools and methods are perennially useful for problem-solving, the ability to draw on Toyota as a source and make effective use of them could be limited or somehow less attractive in the future.

19. The model for Lean was Toyota. Lean does not recognize or acknowledge its Scientific Management heritage. The creators of Lean seem to have made a conscious effort to ignore the legacy of Scientific Management and its influence in creating TPS and the Toyota Way, and hence they distance Lean from it.

20. The myriad forms of Lean management that range from weak to mid-range strength obviously embody many misunderstandings and misapplications of Lean principles and practices. There is no central authority for correcting these problems. They can only be done at the local level if such correction is either needed or desired.

21. This occurred at the Lean Enterprise Institute's 10th Anniversary celebration in Boston in 2007, which the author attended. A focus group recommended the name change from "lean production to "Lean management."

22. It would have been grounds for thorough and complete chastisement of business leaders given the seriousness of the matter in relation to both people's lives and livelihoods and the reputation of Lean management. Leaders' cost-cutting or competitiveness arguments are nullified by the huge sums of money spent on executive compensation and share buy-backs. Perhaps a decision was made to preserve relationships and avoid telling business leaders what to do.

23. In his work, the author (Emiliani) has made the following mistakes (pages 89-91): mistake number 2, 3, 4, 5, 7, 8, and 9.

References

[1] This aphorism is attributed to George Santayana, *The Life of Reason*, 1905, Volume 1, p. 284. See https://en.wikipedia.org/wiki/George_Santayana

[2] Emiliani, B. (2018), *The Triumph of Classical Management Over Lean Management: How Tradition Prevails and What to Do About It*, Cubic LLC, South Kingstown, Rhode Island

[3] Emiliani, B. (2020), *Irrational Institutions: Business, Its Leaders, and The Lean Movement*, Cubic LLC, South Kingstown, Rhode Island

[4] Emiliani, B. (2020), *Management Mysterium: The Quest for Progress*, Cubic LLC, South Kingstown, Rhode Island

[5] Taylor, F. W. (1947), "Taylor's Testimony Before the Special House Committee" in *Scientific Management: Comprising Shop Management, Scientific Management, Testimony Before the Special House Committee*, Foreword by H. S. Person, Harper and Row Publishers, New York, New York ("Testimony of Mr. Frederick Winslow Taylor," *Hearings Before Special Committee of the House of Representatives to Investigate the Taylor and Other Systems of Shop Management Under Authority of H. Res. 90*, Volume 3, 25 January 1912, pp. 1377-1378)

[6] Taylor, F. W. (1911), *The Principles of Scientific Management*, Harper and Brothers, New York, New York, p. 131

[7] Reference 5, p. 1387

[8] Tilman R. (1995), "Thorstein Veblen: Science, Revolution and the Persistence of Atavistic Continuities" in Clark C.M.A. (eds) *Institutional Economics and the Theory of Social Value: Essays in Honor of Marc R. Tool*, Springer, Dordrecht. https://doi.org/10.1007/978-94-011-0655-9_15

[9] Evans, H. (1911), *Cost Keeping and Scientific Management*, McGraw-Hill Book Company, New York, New York

[10] Leffingwell, W. (1917), *Scientific Office Management*, A.W. Shaw Co., New York, New York

[11] Hysell, H. (1922), *The Science of Purchasing*, D. Appleton and Company, New York, New York

[12] Reference 6, page 8

[13] Reference 6, page 26

[14] Reference 5, pages 1388-1389

[15] Haber, S. (1964), *Efficiency and Uplift: Scientific Management and the Progressive Era 1890-1920*, University of Chicago Press, Chicago, Illinois, pp. 16-17

[16] Thompson, C. B. (1917), *The Taylor System of Scientific Management*, A. W. Shaw Company, New York New York

[17] Toyota Motor Corporation (1988), *Toyota: A History of the First 50 Years*, Toyota Motor Corporation, Toyota City, Japan

[18] Wada K. and Yui, T. (2002), *Courage and Change: The Life of Kiichiro Toyoda*, Toyota Motor Corporation, Toyota City, Japan. Translated by Edmund R. Skrzypczak

[19] Ohno, T. (1988), *Toyota Production System – Beyond Large-Scale Production*, Productivity Press, Portland, Oregon, pp. 6-7

[20] Sugimori, Y., Kusunoki, K., Cho, F. and Uchikawa, S. (1977), "Toyota Production System and Kanban System Materialization of Just-in-Time and Respect-for-Human System," *International Journal of Production Research*, Volume 15, No. 6, pp. 553-564

[21] Reference 19, p. xiii

[22] Reference 19, p. xv

[23] Shinohara, I. (1988), *NPS: New Production System: JIT Crossing Industry Boundaries,* Productivity Press, Cambridge, MA, Chapter 13: "A Conversation with the Supreme Advisor, Taiichi Ohno," pp. 153 and 155

[24] Day, P. (2007), "'Mr Toyota' is shy about being No 1," *BBC News,* http://news.bbc.co.uk/2/hi/business/6237110.stm, 25 June, accessed 25 October 2020

[25] Stewart T. and Raman, A. (2007), "Lessons from Toyota's Long Drive," *Harvard Business Review*, July-August, p. 80

[26] Cho, F. (2012), "75 Years of Toyota," http://www.toyota-global.com/company/history_of_toyota/75years/message/index.html, November, accessed 25 October 2020

[27] Greimel, H. (2013), "Toyota's new offensive's goal: Improvement, not sheer volume," *Automotive News*, 11 November, https://www.autonews.com/article/20131111/OEM02/311119994/toyota-s-new-offensive-s-goal-improvement-not-sheer-volume, accessed 25 October 2020

[28] Toyoda, A. "The Toyota Global Vision," https://www.toyota-global.com/pages/contents/company/message_from_president/speech110309.pdf, accessed 25 October 2020

[29] Womack, J., Jones, D., and Roos, D. (1990), *The Machine that Changed the World*, Rawson Associates, New York, New York, pp. 3-9

[30] Krafcik, J.F. (1988), "Triumph of the Lean Production System," *Sloan Management Review*, Vol. 30, No. 1, pp. 41-52

[31] Reference 29, p. 13

[32] Womack, J. and Jones, D. (1996), *Lean Thinking: Banish Waste and Create Wealth in Your Corporation: The Story of Lean Production*, Simon & Schuster, New York, New York

[33] Monden, Y. (1983), *Toyota Production System: Practical Approach to Production Management,* First Edition, Engineering and Management Press, Norcross, Georgia, p. 2

[34] "What is Lean," (2020), Lean Enterprise Institute, Cambridge, Massachusetts, https://www.lean.org/WhatsLean/, accessed 26 October 2020

[35] "The Toyota Way 2001," (2001), Internal Document, Global Human Resources Division, Toyota Motor Corporation, Toyota City, Japan, April

[36] "Toyota Production System" (1992), Toyota Motor Corporation, Internal Public Affairs Division, Operations Management Consulting Division, Toyota City, Japan, April, p. vii

[37] "The Toyota Production System: Leaner Manufacturing for a Greener Planet," (1998), Toyota Motor Corporation, Internal Public Affairs Division, Operations Management Consulting Division, Toyota City, Japan, April, p. v

[38] Reference 19, pp. 14, 15, 73

[39] Woollard, F. G. and Emiliani, B. (2009), *Principles of Mass and Flow Production*, 55th Anniversary Special Reprint Edition, The CLBM, LLC, Wethersfield, Connecticut (Original date of publication of *Principles of Mass and Flow Production*: 1954)

[40] Womack, J. (2007), "Respect for People," eLetter to the LEI community, 20 December, http://www.lean.org/womack/DisplayObject.cfm?o=755, accessed 27 October 2020

[41] Womack, J.P. (2008), "The Toyota concept of 'respect for people," *Reliable Plant*, January, https://www.reliableplant.com/Read/9818/toyota, accessed 27 October 2020

[42] "Toyota CSR Policy" Corporate Social Responsibility Contribution for Sustainable Development, https://global.toyota/en/sustainability/csr/policy/, accessed 27 October 2020.

[43] Source: Stacy Gleiss, a.k.a. The Six-Foot Bonsai, interpreter for Toshihiro Nagamatsu, June 2016

[44] Ohno, T. and Mito, S. (1988), *Just-In-Time For Today and Tomorrow*, Productivity Press, Cambridge, Massachusetts, p. xii

[45] Craig, D. and Charters, W (1925), *Personal Leadership in Industry*, McGraw Hill Book Company, New York, New York

[46] Tead, O. (1935), *The Art of Leadership: What Leadership Is; What Makes a Leader; How Leaders Function; How to Develop Leadership*, McGraw Hill Book Company, New York, New York

[47] Emiliani, M. L. (1998), "Lean Behaviors," *Management Decision*, Vol. 36, No. 9, pp. 615-631

[48] Toussaint, J. and Barnas, K. (2020), *Becoming the Change: Leadership Behavior Strategies for Continuous Improvement in Healthcare*, McGraw Hill Education, New York, New York

[49] Anderson, K. (2020), *Learning to Lead, Leading to Learn: Lessons from Toyota Leader Isao Yoshino on a Lifetime of Continuous Learning*, Integrand Press, San Francisco, California

[50] Dodge, J. M. (1912), "The Spirit in Which Scientific Management Should be Approached," *Scientific Management: First Conference at the Amos Tuck School at Dartmouth College*, 12-14 October 1911, Plimpton Press, Norwood Massachusetts, p. 145

[51] Nakane, J. and Hall, R (2002), "Ohno's Method: Creating a Survival Work Culture," *Target*, Vol. 18, No. 1, pp. 6-15

3
The Improvement Mindset

The Improvement Mindset

Too often the mindset of improvement that people gain upon exposure to progressive management is nothing more than a small extension of their current mindset about improvement. It typically means that people learn some new tools for problem-solving that are better than the problem-solving tools that they used in the past. Furthermore, they succeed in making an improvement, possibly significant, and then often walk away from it – they do not think about how to improve the improvement, and then how to improve the new improvement. Despite knowledge of the words "continuous improvement," improvement tends to be more one-time than it is continuous.

In fairness, there may be some difficulty moving forward with additional improvement due to preconceptions held by leaders in which some improvement is good enough, and more improvement is not needed because too much change upsets the status quo (e.g. investments in existing machines, systems, and processes) and is thus undesirable [1-4]. The training may be poor or one's influential peers may re-shape local understanding of improvement to that which is closer to existing norms. Thus, the inability to grasp the meaning of improvement can have internal or external origins, or a combination of the two.

Recall the words of Henry Gantt:

> "The usual way of doing a thing
> is always the wrong way."

and the words of Akio Toyoda:

> "...we at Toyota are people 'who believe there is always a better way.'"

The two ideas, rooted in experience, not theory, strains peoples' comprehension and their abilities. But that is exactly the idea behind these two quotes. People underestimate their intellectual and creative abilities by huge margins. Poor grades in school, criticism from current or past bosses, or other forms of negative feedback cause people to lose confidence in their intellectual abilities. So, they hew to whatever the norms happen to be and decide it is best to compromise and do what they are told to do. Their critical thinking skills atrophy as does their dignity. Their conception of creativity is narrow and limited to visual arts, literary arts, and performing arts – painting, poetry, music, and like forms of human expression. Most people do not see themselves as creative, even though they engage in hobbies – cooking, gardening, photography, etc. – where they apply creativity in different ways People have ideas, lots of ideas, that come from their innate intellectual and creative abilities, which comes to life in their hobbies.

Classically management organizations seek to suppress human intellectual and creative abilities because it will invariably challenge the status quo in search of change. Such change is permitted, in varying degrees, to the parts of an organization that design, market, and sell products and services. Others typically experience less intellectual and creative freedom. Overall, the levels of intellectual and creative capability in such organizations, where leaders think and workers do, is well below that which is achievable. And this is the problem that is recognized in progressive management. For an organization to grow and survive, it needs the intellectual and creative capabilities of all its people. Yet the construction of classical and neoclassical economics is such that there is no need for the long-term survival of a business. Whether to survive or not is a choice made by leaders, and the choice they usually make is to sell the business if the price is right. Whether the business survives in the hands of its new owner is immaterial. Leaders can also choose to close part or all of a business if it is more profitable to do so. In classical management businesses are nothing more than properties to be bought, sold, or closed to gain advantages in the marketplace for some indeterminate period time. Employees' intellectual and creative abilities, underutilized as they are, have only temporary and disposable value. As a result, training is more a function of business expediency than it is employee development.

Despite an economic construction that is hostile to people and which can even be hostile to business itself, progressive management can prosper in such an environment. But whether it exists in good form depends upon how it is understood by leaders and followers alike. Leaders' understanding of progressive management plays a particularly important role because, through their talk and actions, they establish the norms that people conform to. Leaders can make people or break people; they can grow people or destroy people. Progressive management seeks to do the former, while classical management is more adept at achieving the latter. In progressive management, the assumption, validated long ago by reality, is that business exists in an ever-changing world. As such, it requires continuous adjustments based on sensory perceptions, which in turn, demand that intellectual and creative abilities be constantly exercised and strengthened. Awareness of change must be heightened, and critical thinking skills must be further developed and improved (see Note 1). Problem-awareness and problem-solving are the twin motivators for survival through the practice of progressive management.

It seems that most people view progressive management merely as something similar to classical management, not as that which is completely new; a different species of management thinking and practice with its own distinctive origins and evolutionary path (see Figure 2-1). Interbreeding between these two species, classical management (fish) and progressive management (bird) is not possible. Yet, some leaders skilled in classical management try, but what they get is not much more than what they have always been; likely a fortuitous outcome given their preference the status quo. So, what is progressive management beyond the definition given in the beginning pages of this book? And what is the mindset the forms the foundation of contemporary progressive management? Let's again learn from the past.

For something to be truly new it must possess some creative and innovative characteristics that are broadly recognized as such. Scientific Management was an outgrowth of earlier efforts to improve the then-current chaotic, unsystematic classical management practice ("rule of thumb"). The contribution was "systemization" of repetitive managerial work – a more orderly and consistent directing and controlling of the existing work methods, but no major changes in how the work is done [5]. Essentially, the establishment of procedures or sequence of procedures (documentation) to aid in controlling the work as the scale and complexity of business grew, inclusive of higher customer demand. While systemization improved business efficiency, it did not result in any significant change in thinking.

Scientific Management was the next step in the evolution of progressive management. It was a big step because embodied creativity and innovation in ways that fundamentally changed people's way of thinking about both the role of management and how employees do their work. Moving forward to the late 1940s, Toyota employees apply their own unique forms of creativity and innovation in ways that *again* fundamentally changed people's way of thinking about both the role of management and how employees do their work. The growing use of machine technologies by business will in the future likely lead to a third fundamental change in people's way of thinking about management and work. But for now, we must focus on the second change in people's way of thinking brought to us by Toyota.

In 1981, three years after his retirement from Toyota Motor Corporation, Taiichi Ohno and some colleagues formed a management consulting company in Japan called "NPS Research Association." NPS is an acronym for "New

Production System" [6]. The purpose of the research association was to take the concept of just-in-time across industry boundaries and boundaries within organizations. It was to extend TPS to new frontiers and improve corporate (not just production) efficiency. Member companies, which numbered about 50 in 1985, were led by presidents eager for change (see Note 2). It is not known what happened to the NPS Research Association. But a few years later, a management consulting company was formed not by Mr. Ohno but at his behest, whose purpose was to bring TPS and kaizen to the world. The name of the company was "Shingijutsu," which means new (*shin*) technology (*gijutsu*). The name of both consultancies begins with "new" as in something that is original or innovative, recent in origin or novel, whereas "technology" means practical human skills and capabilities.

Yet the meaning runs deeper. It means to make things new again and again, continuously new, making new never-ending by eliminating abnormalities through practical, human-based methods and skills [7]. In context, "Shingijutsu" means "new management technology," TPS, created via kaizen, a unique and creative form of rapid problem solving based on the discovery of the facts via scientific thinking for the practical purpose of business improvement. Kaizen is the fundamental process that results in the "new management technology," a trial and error method utilizing scientific reasoning processes such as hypothesis testing, induction, deduction, and cause-and-effect. Kaizen is not simply process improvement, but the utilization of human intelligence and creativity to think rationally, innovate, and invent as curious craftsmen would do throughout their working life. And do this without the money and other resources that are so plentiful in classical management. Kaizen develops a new mindset, an improvement mindset, a new and different species of management thinking and practice.

In his book, *Toyota Production System*, Taiichi Ohno said [8]:

> "True innovation – I mean real technological innovation – also brings some kind of social reform."

In this sense, it is a human technology, based on thinking and creativity, evolving over time and generating wisdom, not machine technology that merely does what it is designed to do until it becomes obsolete. It is worth considering the implications of a new management technology in relation to social change and in contrast to machine technology and the institution of leadership. Specifically, how it does or does not lead to change and improvement.

In classical management, the institution of leadership has preconceptions that either favor or disfavor certain types of technological advancement. Disfavoring of technological advancement inhibits technological insights and inventions or contaminates them sufficiently to reduce the magnitude of their impact and align them more closely with the status quo. The status quo being the node around which leaders' goals coalesce. In other words, the introduction of new technological insights and inventions must be consistent with the goals prescribed by the institution of leadership. This decision to obstruct or sabotage new technology is based on the potential loss of power more than the gains that could accrue to leader's goals and interests (see Note 3). The concern is whether a pecuniary gain comes at the expense of social hierarchical relations. Thus, leaders can be in favor of certain technologies and against others, both of which promise to improve business efficiency and pecuniary gain – but one of which forces them to incur other costs that run counter to the demands of the institution of leadership [1-4].

When leaders decide what technology to invest in, they consider four questions:

- Will it force top leaders to change how they do their work?
- Will it force employees to change how they do their work?
- Will it reduce the amount of labor or replace hand labor?
- Can we afford it?

To make the investment, the answers to these four questions must be: no, yes, yes, and yes (see Notes 4 and 5). Obviously, leaders favor technologies that require nothing from them other than their approval. That means near-automatic approval for new *machine* technologies that improves labor efficiency. This preserves the prevailing order as required by the institution of leadership and strengthens leader's power and control over work methods and the organization overall. Looking at this from the opposite direction, leaders do not see new *management* technology as being compatible with the logic of business, wherein the favored means of producing pecuniary gains is expediency. Introducing a new management technology upsets vested interests and the favored status-quo mindset. Furthermore, the typical leader possesses an abstract conception of business as a cash-generating *machine* that is operated by manipulating a universally common set of levers. The decades-long accumulated training and socialization to think in terms of hierarchies, money, budgets, machines, etc., generally precludes viewing new management technology as something that would be beneficial. In fact, the opposite view is widely held that new management technology is harmful to the passions and interests of leaders and the pecuniary ends of business. This logic hinders the rate of improvement and technological change and assures a widening gap between the needs of business and the needs of society as time passes.

Progressive management is often characterized as a socio-technical system, in contrast to classical management which is more the form of a social system – hence the requirement to preserve power, vested interests, etc. Progressive management's practical goal is to replace the above-described habituation and leadership-by-right with a new mindset that is based on facts and which closes the gap between the needs of business and the needs of society. However, its technological superiority over classical management does not automatically make it the winning choice. Classical management is socially and technologically inefficient both on its face and because of the existence of a viable alternative that functions more efficiently within the capitalist system. Classical management is also economically inefficient in that it is not the least-cost method of management.

If the purpose of business is the efficient transformation of input resources to outputs for-profit (or non-profit), yet leaders' choice in decision-making favors preserving one's power and the status quo, then that choice can be reasonably expected to interfere with that purpose given the ever-changing business environment. If, instead, leaders' choice in decision-making is aligned with that purpose, then they would favor progress and improvement. What is the mindset of such a leader? And how does one overcome traditional ways of thinking and learn this mindset, whether or not they are a leader?

Let's begin with the mindset. The following pages give examples of various ways of thinking peculiar to Toyota's management thinking and practice [7], with added context and explanation to help readers' comprehension. It will be described in the no-nonsense voice of a teacher who has had the lived experience of new management technology and destroyed their preconceptions. The examples are presented according to the following categories: People, Process, Equipment, Space, Money, Time, and Information. This is a matter of convenience, not how someone would learn the mindset. In the workplace, these would be learned in combination with one another by participating in improvement activities – specifically, kaizen.

1. People

Respect operators by eliminating their burdens.

The people who do the work of satisfying customer demand have a difficult job. You forgot this because you live in an office. The way the work has been designed is burdensome and unpleasant. If you did their job, you would not like it. You would quit. So do your job as a manager, or anyone else who supports this work, and quickly eliminate operators' burdens. By doing this, you show that you respect them as human beings and that you are interested in them and their work. You must you do all you can to help them be successful in their work. You must emotionally connect to workers and together improve the work.

Kaizen should come from operators' complaints.

Complaints reflect operators' dedication to their job. Do not ignore complaints. Their complaints are a source of improvement ideas. Ignoring operator's complaints shows that you do not care about them and their work. And you fall behind as a company because of your inaction. Being a manager means listening to operators and taking swift action on their complaints. Anyone can ignore operators. You must not do that. Let your competitors do that.

Kaizen is not for cutting jobs. Use wisdom and ingenuity to protect people's lives.

Improvement is for the betterment of the business and its employees, not for the betterment of the business at the expense of employees. Anyone can cut jobs; there is no intelligence in that. There is no creativity or ingenuity in cutting jobs. You are an irresponsible leader if you fail to protect people's lives and livelihoods. You do not respect people when you use kaizen the wrong way. When you use kaizen the wrong way, everything stops. No more improvement. You fall behind and risk losing everything.

You don't need what you think you need.

Every time a problem occurs you say you need something; you need money, people, equipment, software. What you need is to use your brain to think of many different ways to solve problems and try them all out quickly to see which works best. You must wrack your brain for ideas instead of taking the easy way out. You do not develop your intelligence and skills by taking the easy way out. You must accept the effort that is required to overcome your bad habits. If improvement comes easily then you have not made enough effort or improvement.

You have to struggle to squeeze your intelligence out.

Stop looking to other people for answers to your problems. You have intelligence and creativity, but you don't know how to use it. It sits immobile in your brain like a sea urchin. When you are hungry you have no problem thinking of ways to feed yourself. But you are helpless when you have problems at work. You want to relax and have things come easily to you. Why does anyone give you a job? You can relax at home. At work you must struggle to make things better. You cannot be soft on yourself.

Generate intelligence instead of generating waste.

Your school education robbed you of your intelligence.

When you copy people doing things the old way you become a willing accomplice in their crime of stealing your intelligence. You only know how to generate waste. You are only worth what you are paid if you generate intelligence. Otherwise you are overpaid. You have a responsibility to the company to use all your intelligence to eliminate waste. You must immediately regain your curiosity and apply your intelligence by questioning everything.

Think by doing. Don't start thinking before doing.

When you think before doing, you talk yourself out of doing many things and instead focus on doing one or two things; one or two ideas. Those might be the worst ideas because they are the easiest for you to do and the least effective. You did not challenge yourself. You again took the easy way. Just start trying things out. Try as many things as you can and learn from them all. From that will come a solution as well as wisdom from having tried many things.

2. Process

No abnormality is an abnormality.

If nothing is wrong, if there are no problems, then that is a problem. Every aspect of business has problems at all times. How can there be no problems? You are a bad manager if you have no problems. You lack curiosity and ignore reality if you think you have no problems. This attitude means you are lazy and afraid. You're fired! You will be rehired immediately if you start recognizing problems as soon as they occur and use your intelligence and get your hands dirty to solve problems with your team.

The truth lies only where work is performed.

You sit in an office all day and think you know what is going on. Why do you fool yourself this way? It must make you feel better. But you are at work and you should not feel better; you should feel pain – the pain of people who do the work. Get out of your office and go to where the work is done. Stand there and see what is going on. If you like what you see, then you are blind. You are not dumb, but you need to become a lot smarter. You cannot lead people if you don't know what they are doing and how they are struggling. Observe what is happening and use your intelligence to improve the work.

Processes should be people-centered with simple house-made equipment as-needed.

You always want to buy complex machines and do not care about how people are affected. Does the machine generate problems for operators? Figure out the process first. Make it people-centered. Then if machines are needed, they must be simple to operate. Make the machines in house. This way people build their skills and capabilities. They learn new things and gain confidence and are able to do more in the future. People have fun building simple machines. It builds teamwork and costs less than buying machines from companies that want to sell you more machine than you need. You want lower costs, right? Buy only the machines, or parts of machines, that you cannot build yourselves.

Why don't you think to improve it 10 times as much?

Everyone thinks to improve something 5 or 10 or 15 percent. Why do you think like everyone else? What is the point in that, other than to put you behind? Think how to improve it 5 or 10 or 15 times as much. This forces you to rethink everything and use your intelligence. It creates dire conditions that have no answer with traditional thinking. So you must think differently; be creative and develop breakthrough ideas to try. Work together with your team and you will succeed much sooner than you think.

Lift or move things with one finger.

You walk by and don't notice people struggling to lift or move things around by hand or with expensive equipment. You see this terrible situation and think it is normal. It is not. It is abnormal. You do not challenge yourself to think of ways to move or lift things with one finger, or devise ways that things can move by themselves. You need to dream of the impossible and then turn it into practical reality. That is how you put distance between yourself and your competition.

This is not to make work harder. It is to make work simpler.

It is easy to make work hard and to make things more complex. Everybody does that. Why do you do what everybody does? Does it make you feel happy or more satisfied? It's not right to make people suffer. Throughout history humans try to make work easier. How come in your company everything is so hard? Doesn't that create endless opportunities for errors and rework? What makes you think you have money for that? You must make work simpler. It will cost less. It will make people happier. Your customers will be happier.

What is the purpose of being born and being here if you do re-work or fix people's mistakes?

Just because you pay somebody does not mean it is right for them to come to work every day to do re-work or fix people's mistakes. Why is this considered acceptable? When you waste their time you waste their lives. You have no right to do that. Does anyone ask for that? People want their work to have meaning. You should apologize and stop doing it immediately. Don't be afraid to apologize.

3. Equipment

Engineers get tricked by machine manufacturers.

Engineers like to look at catalogs and buy things. When they meet with salespeople they fall in love with the machine and add more things to the machine so they can love it even more. The people who sell machines know this and so they have many tricks to increase the engineers' love. Engineer's school education has failed them. They should buy only what they need in the machine and use their ingenuity to finish building the machine to perform only the necessary function. Engineers also get tricked by software makers. Buy only the software needed to perform the necessary function if you cannot make it yourself.

Everyone has similar machines. It is how you use the machines that makes the difference.

Machines are similar in any industry. They are similar because everyone's thinking is similar. Sometimes there is no other choice. But how you use the machine makes a difference. Are you using it professionally, or using it like an amateur? Does it suit the process you designed, or are you using a machine that can do more than what is needed? Is it doing a specific operation on a specific item? Is it located in the workflow or outside the workflow? Just because you buy a machine does not mean you are done. You must figure out how to use it correctly.

Machines should be quiet. Operators should not wear earplugs.

Why do you accept all the noise here? Don't you have any curiosity to understand the cause of this noise? You work in a quiet office, but operators have to put up with this noise all day. You disrespect workers by ignoring all the noise. You need to care about workers and do something to eliminate this noise. Have a team investigate and make improvements. Work with the equipment manufacturer if necessary. Tell them you won't buy equipment from them anymore if they don't help you fix it.

Build equipment that suits the process you design.

People spend too much money buying more equipment than they need with many more features than they need. Design the process first and then figure out what equipment is needed. Make sure it is no larger than necessary and can fit in the workflow. Make the equipment in-house to develop your engineering and process capabilities. Do not rely on outsiders for your processes and process knowledge.

Computers kill your ability to think.

Be careful with computers. You spend too much time in front of them and not enough time with workers thinking about abnormalities and how to make improvements. You no longer have the ability to sketch by hand or do hand calculations. You must recover these lost skills. Otherwise, you will be like everyone else relying on the same equipment for the same problems and come up with the same answers that the computer tells you. When you listen to what the computer tells you, you allow it to steal your intelligence. Why would you allow such a thing to happen?

4. Space

Throw this out! Get rid of this!

Every time you get more orders from customers you want to increase the size of building or break ground on a new building. Why do you do such a thing? You say you want low costs, but you keep increasing costs. Just because bankers say you have the money to do it does not mean you should. Stop staring at the computer and making calculations. Use your eyes to see what surrounds you. The building is full of things that you do not need. Throw them out to make space for doing productive work. Keep only what is needed for today and tomorrow.

Close the warehouse!

Why do you have this warehouse? It is because the way you make things is not in line with your customer's demand. You are disconnected from the marketplace. You make too much of something and then have to store it and hope it sells. It costs money to store things. You pay taxes on stuff that sits around doing nothing. Maybe you discount it to get rid of it and lose profit. Maybe it becomes obsolete and you lose all the money you spent. Is that any way to run a business? Take down the shelves and empty this warehouse. You do not need this space. Rent it out to someone else and make some money. Sell the warehouse to someone who lacks intelligence like you once did. Let them believe stagnation is a good business plan. You must learn how to produce to the rate of customer demand. Locate small quantities of inventory where the items are made, at the end of the line, and withdraw finished goods from there.

Offices and cubicles are like jail cells. What did people do wrong to get treated like that?

Small errors lead to big problems. Office and cubicles seem like a good idea because you see other companies with offices and cubicles. Why do you blindly copy others? You must think for yourself. Offices and cubicles are barriers to people working together. Break down those barriers so that people communicate better, so you know about problems sooner, so problems can be corrected immediately. Make the environment so that information flows freely. Do things to improve teamwork, not make teamwork harder.

Reduce the distance between process steps.

Why is there so much space between steps in the process? Is this space free? Do you get a discount in rent or taxes for empty space? You can produce two or three times more in this space. Put each step next to the other from start to finish, using equipment that is not larger than height or width of a human body. If what you are making is big in size, apply the same concept. This way you will use space more efficiently and the operators can work together.

5. Money

It feels good to spend money. Stop it!

You always talk about costs being too high, but then find a way to spend more money. It must feel good to spend money. Why else would you do it? You are in business. It is difficult to make profit. So you must stop spending money. Spend ideas instead. If spending makes you feel good, then spend your own money at home, not company money at work. You are stealing from the company when you spend its money instead of spending ideas. Spend ideas first. Use intelligence instead of money. Only after you have squeezed out all your intelligence are you allowed to spend the company's money.

Owners' financial vision far exceeds their actual financial condition.

You look at your accounts and think everything is good. And you think business will pick up in the future. But what if it does not? Because you are optimistic you have loaded yourself with debt in anticipation of future business. Owners get tricked by bankers. Is that debt free? No, you pay principal and interest. Interest may be cheap, but it is still money that you must pay. Your actual financial condition is dire because you look more at bank accounts than what is happening in production. You risk the company and put your employees and customers at risk. How can you do such a thing? I hear businesspeople are conservative. Your financial condition is more like someone who became rich overnight and wastes money. Your pay should be cut for mismanaging the company (see Note 6).

Don't buy things you have to pay taxes on. Make it yourself.

It is easy to buy equipment, furniture, and other expensive things. You are always thinking about what to buy. Employees tell you they need the company to buy things. So you are always buying expensive things. Because you can amortize the expense you think it is a wise purchase. But it is not. You still pay for it, and you must also pay taxes on it. When you do that you increase costs and do not learn anything. So you have failed in two ways. Learn from your mistakes. Make what you need using inexpensive parts that you can expense rather than capitalize. Build internal skills and capabilities. Think about how to design processes for low taxes both in terms of equipment and output.

To get paid as professional, you have to apply intelligence to make things better.

When you do things as other people do, you are thinking like an amateur. Merely copying others is amateur skill level. You are paid as a professional, so you must think like a professional. You must apply your intelligence to make things better than how other people do things. Otherwise, the company can fire you and hire amateurs and pay them less. There is no need to pay you so much. The company should give you a big pay cut. When you become a professional the company can increase your pay. Yesterday you received a paycheck that was for work you did two weeks ago. Did you do anything in the last two weeks to make things better? What will you do in the next two weeks to make things better? Professionals always think about how to make or do something better. Why aren't you doing that?

6. Time

Measure time with a stopwatch, in seconds.

How long does it take to do this? You don't know. You can only give me an estimate. That is a guess. But I timed it and your estimate was off by 152 percent. You cannot run a business by guessing how long it takes to do things. You give prices to customers based on how much time it takes to do the work. But your guesses are almost never correct. Your guesses are either too long, and so you lose business, or too short and so you lose money. Is that any way to run a business? You have learned the skill of how to go broke. Why are you paid to ruin a business? Measure time with a stopwatch, in seconds. Then apply intelligence to eliminate the queue time and balance the cycle times so that you can earn more profit, grow, and survive.

Just because the customer gives you a lot of time does not mean you should take it.

Business needs customers, but customers can sometimes mislead you or lull you into complacency. If a customer gives you 30 days to fill an order, you think the customer thinks 30 days is acceptable. That may be, but things change. One day they will surprise you and want it in 20 days or 15 days or 10 days. And because you designed the process for 30 days, you lose business. Have you not been thinking how your customers' business may change? You have not anticipated customer needs that are predictable. As time passes, people want to wait less. They want what they want sooner. So why do you run a business that is stagnant in how long it takes to get work done? You must always think about how to improve processes so they flow and take less time. You should never speed people up. Instead, you must use intelligence and creativity to change the process so that it is simpler, easier, and also takes less time.

Try things quickly.

You want to control everything. This is because you are afraid of mistakes. But you have already made a big mistake. You must think about what needs to be controlled versus the things you want to control but which do nothing but create impediments to improvement. You want to review and approve everything. That's no good. It causes long delays in taking action when problems arise. Brainstorming also causes long delays. When problems arise, think of many ideas to try quickly before the workday ends. Do only trystorming. Don't do brainstorming. Make progress quickly because your customers want better products and services and no problems. They want all of these things now, not next month or next year.

I want you to cut a digit from that number, 360 seconds. Do it in 36 seconds.

It takes 360 seconds to do that. You tell me that your goal is 300 seconds, a 17 percent improvement. To you that seems like a big improvement. Why are you satisfied with that? It is because you are used to small gains in efficiency. You learned that in school and from other people at work. When you let others think for you, you will never imagine the amount of improvement that is possible. I want you to make ten-times improvement. Find a way to do it 36 seconds. When you succeed, you will wonder why you ever did it in 360 seconds. You will also wonder why everyone thinks 17 percent improvement is a big achievement when it is not. You will have found 324 seconds per item of time that can be used to fill customer orders. You will not be behind schedule anymore, the company can look for higher sales of that product, and the product is now more profitable. Stop thinking the way everyone else does. There is no benefit to doing that.

7. Information

When you physically do it, your hands will think for you.

There is no progress here because you always try things out in your head, not with your hands. When you try things out in your head you make a judgement of what will work or not work. That judgement will be wrong in some way. Either it will work when you thought it would not, or you exclude ideas that should be tried because they seem far-fetched. You must not limit yourself. Even if you don't think it will work, try it anyway. I want you to connect your brain to your hands. Get your hands dirty and try it out. Do something with your hands: make a cardboard mock-up, move equipment around, make a fixture, rearrange things in different order, make some sketches. You will think better when your brain and hands are connected. It develops your intelligence. The improvements you make will be better and many times it will be a big breakthrough. Let your competitors think with their head and let them believe they are better than you. Soon they will learn who is better, but they will not know why.

One cannot understand the true facts from an office desk or report.

You are fooled into thinking that you know what is going on by looking at computer screens and reports. If you rely on this information for decision-making you will make many mistakes and ruin the company. You don't know how the computer information is produced. You assume it is accurate. How do you know? The most important information is the facts. This comes from the place where the work is done. Go there to observe what is happening. Talk to the operators and find out their complaints and struggles. In the beginning you will not understand what you are looking at because you do not have eyes for it. You only have eyes for computer screens and reports. You let information come to you. You always take the easy way. Go get the facts that are required for you to make good decisions. Go to the workplace and learn to see what is actually happening. You must do this every day. Soon you will see 1000 things needing improvement. Only then will you be a professional manager.

Inconvenient information will never surface.

Bad news does not come to you because people are afraid of consequences. So you have to go get the bad news yourself. You find it by going to the workplace and observing what is happening. Look for abnormalities. Talk to workers. You must thank workers when they give you inconvenient information, so they give you more in the future. If you do not seek out this information, you will make bad decisions and those bad decisions will make things worse. Soon you will have really big problems. So do not delay. Go get inconvenient information every day so problems do not build up.

People give too much information all at once. People are busy and have many things on their mind. They are easily distracted. Because they say "yes" or nod their head in agreement does not mean they listened or understood anything. Meetings in conference rooms have long agendas to talk about too many things for too long that are not important. It is just to take up managers' high-paid time and look important. These are bad habits that must be broken. You must always give only the information that is needed, where it is needed, in the amount needed, when it is needed. Do this quickly so that people do not get bored listening to you and can return to their work.

These examples provide an understanding of the mindset of improvement and the rationale for change. It is the mindset of the new management technology that is the core of modern progressive management given to us by Toyota. It is the expression of a curiosity-driven, fact-based way of thinking that constitutes a significant advancement over the improvement mindset developed during the days of Scientific Management. In certain ways it is clearer and more exacting, yet in other ways it is more open-ended and flexible to accommodate changing circumstances. Its sensibility is apparent to those who appreciate newness and uniqueness grounded in facts, and highly questionable to those who harbor suspicions about these same things.

It leads the former to wipe away worker stereotypes and organize sustained training and education, and the latter to push people who favor facts out of the way. It begs the questions, "what is leadership?" and "who should lead?" The guardians of the status quo? Or others who understand the difference between traditions that are worth keeping and those that are no longer useful due to changing times.

One cannot help but notice that the voice in previous pages speaks in a sharp, personal tone. Why is that? It is to shake managers out of their complacency and their rigid acceptance of the status quo. Progressive management requires people to be dissatisfied with the status quo sufficiently to question everything and re-think how things should be done more efficiently and more effectively, in ways that are beneficial to people (see Notes 7 and 8). A more diplomatic tone can succeed, but often it fails to make the needed impact. The impact must be on an individual human level, as well as the levels of the company and society. Managers must understand their role and responsibilities as being more significant than just a high-paying job where they are permitted to take the easy way.

The highest paid people should have the least problem with such a tone of communication, but the institution of leadership requires leaders to interpret this tone as nothing but insults. And when that happens, they retreat to the status quo. Managers are not corporate ornaments or decorations. They are part of the workforce whose work of information processing and decision-making is often impaired by intolerance for the facts and what they will reveal (see Notes 9 and 10). This is not the mindset of improvement. It is the mindset of ignorance and irresponsibility hiding behind a façade of knowledge and competence conferred by one's status in a corporate or social hierarchy.

How does one overcome mindset of ignorance and irresponsibility? The one thing that can have the biggest impact is kaizen. In particular, Toyota's kaizen methods [7, 9, 10]. Kaizen, whether practiced individually or by a team, is a remarkable creation. It demands that people face the facts by making problems visible so that improvements can be made. But it does more than that. It brings deeper levels of thinking and restores craftsmanship to one's work. It can be seen as a form of workplace hobby or gamification to stimulate people's curiosity to improve efficiency by eliminating waste. In his book *Toyota Production System*, Taiichi Ohno said [11]:

> "Unless all sources of waste are detected and crushed, success will always be just a dream."

It has often been said that the essence of progressive management is problem-solving and that employees are the source of competitive advantage. These are both true. Yet the true source of strength is finding ways to organize talent at all levels for problem-solving based on the facts, to be adaptive to change through the continuous development of skills and capabilities. In classical management, success depends on a battle of machine technologies between competitors. The human technology is something to tolerate until it can be replaced. Again, that is taking the easy way. Progressive management is more accepting of difficult challenges. Success depends more on human technology than machine technologies – bringing human curiosity, intelligence, and creativity from the recesses of people's minds to the forefront of their work experience.

For this to happen, people must submit to new workplace norms; a new model of what is important and what people should be doing as part of their jobs. Employees must know and feel comfortable that their contributions will not cause them harm in ways such as being sped up, pay cuts, unemployment, or transfer to jobs they cannot do. Bringing intelligence and creativity to the forefront of employees' work involves ongoing training in specific knowledge areas and close supervision with respect to problem-solving, both of which are an anathema in classical management because these are seen as costs with little or no payback. It takes a lot of careful, ongoing thought on how to instill in employees certain ways of thinking and doing things, and to define a large envelope of parameters that helps guide them as times change. Training and organizing to make this happen is a greater achievement than people realize.

Progressive management will change in many ways in the future, but kaizen should be a constant feature of it. This, as well as organizing talent at all levels for fact-based problem-solving, is the most valuable component of Toyota's management practice. To not understand this and not carry it forward into the future seems likely to be a big mistake, one that someone may write about decades from now.

Notes

1. In general, the critical thinking skills that come from K-12 and higher education form, at best, a low baseline of capability. The challenge in progressive management is to raise people's capability for critical thinking (intelligence and creativity) by putting the facts in their face and training them in new problem-solving routines bounded by goals such as eliminating waste and principles such as "continuous improvement" and "respect for people."

2. The Director of the NPS Research Association, Mikiya Kinoshita (former president of Ushio Electric), said this about leaders' objections to improvement: "When we go to companies headed by hired presidents and tell these executives what they're doing is wrong, that they have to shape up, they usually complain that they are being embarrassed in front of the employees, that they have nowhere to go. They don't feel they must put up with a little embarrassment for the good of the company. These presidents are only concerned about their job security or their image. Owner-presidents, on the other hand, don't worry about criticism. If we criticize them, they'll challenge us. They're more driven. I think those are the reasons that our member companies tend to be run by owner-presidents." (Reference 6, pp. 128-129). The suggestion that leaders can and must do better is taken as an insult. The idiom "you can dish it out, but you can't take it" comes to mind. The presumption of equality in this idiom is, of course, offensive to leaders and also taken as an insult.

3. In classical management, the most important criteria in leadership decision-making is whether the decision preserves or increases power. Most leaders are obsessed with gaining leverage over other people or organizations, in part because that is seen as easier for them to achieve than transitioning to a new management technology.

4. Leader will purchase technologies that change how they work only if it results in greater convenience for them.

5. "Yes" to these two questions: "Will it force employees to change how they do their work?" and "Will it reduce the amount of labor or replace hand labor?" reflect owners' demand for wealth accumulation as well as accumulation of property and related rights, and which also results in subordination of workers' interests (such as higher wage or improved work conditions). See Figure 2-2.

6. When it comes to spending money (or saving money), think in terms of pennies, not dollars. When you think this way, the number is much larger, and you might think twice about spending so much money. A machine that costs $1,000,000 actually costs you ¢100,000,000. You can't afford to spend that much money. Your only option is to spend ideas. An employee has a suggestion that will save $100. You ignore the savings because it is not a big number. The actual savings is ¢10,000. That's a lot of money saved! Don't ignore $1 or ¢1 savings. Capture those savings because earning profit is difficult. You cannot afford to let any savings slip through your hands. This is part of the improvement mindset.

7. Opponents of change try to maintain the status quo by arguing that trade-offs are inevitable, and thus there is no way to balance the interests of different parties. This is the mindset of classical management. Experience with progressive management has taught that competing interests can be balanced in the real world – not perfectly so, which nobody asks for anyway, but well enough so that the parties are either reasonably satisfied or at least not disgruntled. Be aware of those who proffer arguments designed to induce cognitive biases (framing, anchoring, status quo, and forecasting) and which employ illogical thinking (false assumptions, avoiding the force of reason, false dilemma, and special pleading).

8. Another argument is that progressive management will cost too much, as if classical management, inefficient and famous for externalizing costs, is intrinsically free of costs. Future generations must aggressively beat back straw man arguments. Yet another argument is that progressive management threatens leaders' freedoms. Yet leaders must not have the freedom or right to harm others. While there is some validity to this argument, the overall gains produced exceed this narrow loss to leaders' freedom.

9. Leaders who exhibit the basic level of bravery expected of them and go seek the facts to understand what is happening on the frontlines (the *genba*) are deeply affected personally and in ways that soon affect their behaviors, corporate policy, and decision-making. For a wonderful example of the sudden changes in perspective that come from interacting with shop and office floor workers, see

Cumberland, D. and Alagaraja, M. (2016), "No Place Like the Frontline: A Qualitative Study on What Participant CEOs Learned From Undercover Boss," *Human Resource Development Quarterly*, Vol. 27, No. 2, pp. 271-296, https://doi.org/10.1002/hrdq.21252

10. Generational differences between top leaders and young workers all but assures a large gap in varied perceptions about people, their motivations, work, and satisfaction. Brave leaders seek to understand and close this gap in the direction of the needs and interests of the younger generation. Corporate culture should evolve in the direction of younger to older. Leaders must not kill the spirit of youth; their wonderful intelligence, curiosity, and creativity.

References

[1] Emiliani, B. (2018), *The Triumph of Classical Management Over Lean Management: How Tradition Prevails and What to Do About It*, Cubic LLC, South Kingstown, Rhode Island

[2] Emiliani, B. (2020), *Irrational Institutions: Business, Its Leaders, and The Lean Movement*, Cubic LLC, South Kingstown, Rhode Island

[3] Emiliani, B. (2020), *Management Mysterium: The Quest for Progress*, Cubic LLC, South Kingstown, Rhode Island

[4] See Appendix I

[5] Litterer, J. (2018), *The Emergence of Systematic Management as Shown by the Literature of Management from 1870-1900*, Routledge Library Editions, New York, New York. Doctoral dissertation of Joseph A. Litterer, Department of Business, University of Illinois, 1959.

[6] Shinohara, I. (1988), *NPS New Production System: JIT Crossing Industry Boundaries*, Productivity Press, Cambridge, Massachusetts

[7] Emiliani, B., Yoshino, K., and Go, R. (2015), *Kaizen Forever: Teachings of Chihiro Nakao*, The CLBM, LLC, Wethersfield, Connecticut

[8] Ohno, T. (1988), *Toyota Production System – Beyond Large-Scale Production*, Productivity Press, Portland, Oregon, p. 91

[9] Wood, R., Herscher, M. and Emiliani, B. (2015), *Shingijutsu-Kaizen: The Art of Discovery and Learning*, The CLBM, LLC, Wethersfield, Connecticut

[10] Kato, I. and Smalley, A. (2011), *Toyota Kaizen Methods: Six Steps to Improvement*, CRC Press, Boca Raton, Florida

[11] Reference 8, p. 59

Final Thoughts

Final Thoughts

Progressive arguments are knocked down, often quite easily, because conservative opponents aggressively present progressivism as an "either-or" choice. Either you are conservative or progressive. In fact, it is both. To the best of my knowledge, every one of the most able practitioners of progressive management were conservative business leaders. What they saw in progressive management was the ability for all employees to see the facts of any matter quickly so that immediate action can be taken, which resulted in less short-, mid-, and long-term risk to the organization. They saw progressive management as reducing chaos and relieving them of the burden of having to know everything and make all the decisions. They saw a more sustainable and balanced path for wealth creation. They saw traditional rights and privileges as barriers to progress. Progressive management allowed them to focus on what they need to know to lead the organization, to focus on the craft of leadership, and make the kinds of decisions that leaders need to make. It allowed them to lead in ways that they could not do otherwise. It is accurate to claim that progressive management, from Scientific Management to the development of Toyota's production system, has evolved in a direction that is more favorable to the passions and interests of conservative business leaders were they not limited by preconceptions and the institution of leadership.

It seems paradoxical that being other-regarding can bear more fruit than being self-regarding. After all, that goes against the teachings of classical and neoclassical economics, or at least how they are commonly interpreted, as well as liberalism and the institution of leadership. People respond positively to leaders who will, in some measure, protect them from the vicissitudes of life, much of which comes from steady employment. This is a reasonable expectation of the role that persons in authority should have, among their other roles. Yet under the aegis of classical management, this role can be difficult to fulfill. It is simply easier for leaders to respond to a favored in-group and ignore facts that cause practical and intellectual difficulties. But eventually a distaste for this grows among those who are in the out-groups. Self-regarding and skepticism of facts will threaten the human experience in varied and unexpected ways. Some leaders will sense a change in their environment and adapt. This too is a reasonable expectation of the role of persons in authority.

Respect for traditions is important. Also important is for leaders to know or sense when the passing of time renders traditions less useful and thus become a barrier to doing what is needed. Progressive management is a change in focus from rights and privileges to duty and service. Some leaders need time to adjust to that, others are less bothered. For all the talk in classical management about efficiency and improvement, the usual basis of decision-making is power or profits – more typically the former because it enables the latter. That is not meant to suggest that these are not important. These ends can be achieved by other means. A more invisible but still ever-present power (*ninjutsu*) and more visible and improved profit outcome. The old order stands to gain by giving way to the new.

One could argue that capitalism and liberalism has failed. Countless books have been written on this topic. But that causality is incorrect. Within this realm there is broad discretion for leaders to manage in ways that can either weaken or strengthen capitalism and liberalism, despite what rapacious laws and customs may allow them to do. Over time, certain traditions, such as the conquering hero, will end up doing more weakening than strengthening, possibly leading to less desirable outcomes. Business leaders crave order, certainty, and simplicity, yet view change as resulting only in disorder, uncertainty, and complexity, as well as loss. Change is not unidirectional in its outcomes.

All of this is to say that there is much common ground between the aims and goals of conservative business leaders and the aims and goals of progressive management. This common ground has yet to be completely understood and productively acted upon.

Classical management will be around for a long time because it makes the best sense to many leaders, despite its strategic vulnerabilities (see Note 1). But their numbers may diminish over time as leaders begin to see the faces of their stakeholders when contemplating decisions, as they begin to realize they don't know all there is to know, and as the need to unlearn what was learned becomes clearer. Harm done to others will likely go from being largely irrelevant to a grand exhibition of pathetic leadership and shameful weakness; the abandonment of one's duties and responsibilities.

The leadership qualities that were once so highly favored

will become the most contemptible. At some point, the desire to tackle unglamorous challenges, such as making needed corrections, will transition from optional to required. Future challenges cannot be met with continued impoverished and sedentary thinking. These challenges require leaders to be critical and creative thinkers and instill that in others. And it requires the establishment of trust to achieve consensus and thus move forward. To some significant degree, perception replaces preconception, *de facto* replaces *de jure*, courage replaces fear, curiosity replaces indifference, originality replaces banality, action replaces indolence, mastery replaces incompetence, simplicity replaces complexity, non-zero-sum replaces zero-sum, and "we" replaces "I" (see Note 2). There may be a renewal in obligations to the company, its stakeholders, and society that have long been ignored. That will include the pursuit of bold, seemingly impossible, new technologies that reverse the problems caused previous generations of technology.

Future leaders of the progressive management movement have their own challenges. The first is that they cannot assume they know the answer to the problem statement:

What methods will result in wider acceptance
for progressive management?

There is no blueprint for that. The second challenge is organizing diverse talent for fact-based problem-solving. The third challenge is embodying the can-do spirit of kaizen to do what seems impossible. To not accept defeat and keep experimenting and trying many new ideas. In pursuing these challenges, one must be mindful of the arguments discussed in Chapter 1, the mistakes presented in Chapter 2, and the improvement mindset described in Chapter 3. To forget these would be to repeat history in ways that one should desperately want to avoid. As was said in the Preface, the "hundred-year plan" must not become a project that is executed according to a detailed project management plan. Instead, a community of interested persons must generate and test many new ideas over time and learn from the various outcomes. These experiments will vary in duration and be some combination of long-term, mid-term, and short-term. The "plan" should be simple: think of many ideas to try, some quickly and some over extended periods of time, and observe the outcomes. Constant creative experimentation and expanded collaboration will generate useful innovations that will help build a better future.

There will always be a need to manage people and a need for people to manage processes, and these should be performed in the most intelligent ways possible (see Note 3). In some cases that will be machine intelligence, in other causes it will be human intelligence. Both will benefit from the application of the mindset of progressive management. Yet one must proceed carefully. Bottom-up demand for change is insulting to classical management leaders because of implicit messages such as: you are not doing a good job, you are behind the times, you care only about yourself, etc. Their identity, formed largely by preconceptions, prevents them from seeing the problems that progressive management addresses.

On the one hand there seems to be a need for diplomacy while on the other hand there seems to be a need for artless candor, if not a duty to intervene because the management practice is complacent and no longer aligns with the views of employees and society. Navigating this dialectic has been and will continue to be a significant challenge, one that needs to be understood as a political problem that requires political solutions [1] – at least in part – but without the stain of partisanship. Somehow a sense of teamwork in pursuit of new or improved shared values and ideals must prevail. This will require a sustained and coordinated effort, more creative use of the internet (e.g. virtual meetings, social media) and new ideas on how to more effectively interact with leaders committed to classical management.

Progressive management thinking has been successful in formulating a "new management technology" practice that is responsive to current and future needs. The question is whether the mistakes presented in Chapter 2 will be corrected or repeated. The mistakes, in some way or another, affect how leaders and workers perceive progressive management. While both must be engaged, the larger opportunity that awaits is with workers and the public. It is especially important to reach younger generations who feel that the logic of prior generations does not address the challenges that affect their lives and the lives of future generations. It would be a mistake to not engage them and their imagination.

The Big Question

You have finished reading this book. Maybe you "got it." You understand the challenge. But, what will you do?

Think of eight ideas. Write the down here:

-
-
-
-
-
-
-
-

About the Cover

The graphic element on the cover of this book is the emblem on the flag of Toyota City, Aichi Prefecture, Japan. Prior to being named "Toyota City," the town was known as *Koromo*, which in Japanese means "clothes" or "garments." Koromo was a center for silk spinning, weaving, and cloth distribution until the late 1930s. The emblem is a stylized version of the kanji character 衣. It is used on the cover as a symbol of creativity, innovation, and improvement both by and for humanity. It reflects the creative and innovative thinking that began with Sakichi Toyoda, followed by Kiichiro Toyoda, and then to Taiichi Ohno and Toyota employees. The creative thinking that Toyota people applied to Scientific Management, which led to producing something greatly improved, in-step with actual market conditions, is remarkable.

Additionally, clothing is a fundamentally human invention that satisfies a basic need. It is a continuous source of innumerable practical creative inventions – spinning, knitting, and weaving machines, and clothing colors, weaves, patterns, designs, and styles.

Finally, the background image on the cover evokes a dreamscape from which creative ideas emerge, or a smooth flow of change or improvement over time.

Notes

1. Classical management's strategic vulnerabilities include population growth, unemployment, healthcare, the environment (externalities), and pecuniary inefficiency. Similar to "energy transition" from carbon to renewable energy, there will emerge a need for "management transition" from classical to progressive.

2. At some point there will be a general recognition of the view that zero-sum classical management "is the best we got" is no longer sustainable. This can happen without resorting to moral evangelism or revolutionary zeal. Improvement lies in finding common cause and common ground with the values and ideals held in high regard by society, while ensuring that those less fortunate are not left behind and that they too realize an array of favorable outcomes. Think "let's find the best of both worlds" rather than "my world is better than yours."

3. Stupidity is not intellectual diversity.

References

[1] Emiliani, B. (2018), *The Triumph of Classical Management Over Lean Management: How Tradition Prevails and What to Do About It*, Cubic LLC, South Kingstown, Rhode Island

Appendix I

Teleological and Ateleological Analysis of Classical, Lean, and Toyota Management Systems and the Lean Movement

Abstract

Examines means-ends in classical and contemporary progressive systems of management using a Western philosophical framework using mixed methods of exploratory, causal, descriptive, qualitative research. It compares and contrasts classical management teleology to Toyota management system ateleology and the mixed ateleology-teleology of Lean management. Recasting these systems in a Western philosophical framework helps to better understand and explain differences between them and how they function in relation to means and ends within the larger system of capitalistic business enterprise where they reside. Research is based on the extant literature, observations in multiple field settings, and the author's firsthand experiences in varied management environments. This is thought to be the first time that teleological and ateleological analysis of classical and contemporary progressive systems of management has been made. The philosophical framework for understanding differences between classical and contemporary progressive systems of management can be used to a) improve the understanding and practice of progressive management systems and b) imagine new strategies and tactics to gain wider CEO acceptance for progressive management.

Introduction

The author's research since 2007 has been largely focused on answering questions that have existed since the time of Scientific Management more than 100 years ago. Advocates of progressive management, from the old Scientific Management to the new Lean management, have persistently had great difficulty in convincing top corporate leaders to replace archaic classical management practice with a new system of progressive management. This has led to 100-plus years of shared frustration among untold numbers of business professionals, and is succinctly captured in this statement (Miner, 2020):

> "I spent 3 years 'selling' lean face to face with CEO's and I'm still mind boggled that my success was so low. They want the results but when you're honest with them about how they need to change their own behavior they say nah, not interested."

In the past this problem has always been addressed at a superficial level (e.g. leader behaviors), resulting in the inability to identify the underlying factors that produce the observed problem – which is that business leaders strongly prefer the status quo when it comes to leadership and management practice. No progress was made in solving this problem for over 100 years because the problem was not understood and thus ill-defined, in part because the problem is far more difficult and complex than was realized. Solving this problem required going outside the contemporary literature of Lean, leadership, management, organizational behavior, psychology, and so on, to identify causal relationships. Namely, a deep dive into economics, sociology, and political science research published between 1890-1925. Recent work provided a comprehensive understanding of why leaders resist or reject Lean management (Emiliani, 2018, 2020, 2020a). These works answered these questions from three different perspectives:

- Why do most top leaders resist or reject Lean management?
- Why do most shop and office floor workers likewise resist or reject Lean management?

But still, some lingering questions remain.

The present work seeks to illuminate the relationship between means and ends in classical management and Lean management compared to Toyota management using a Western philosophical framework. In doing so, it seeks to answer three questions. The first question expands on one of the questions answered in Appendix II:

1. How do the staff of salaried professionals derive satisfaction from their association with Lean management given that progress is so difficult to achieve?

The next two questions pertain to the relationship between means and ends in classical management and Lean management compared to Toyota management:

2. Why does classical management so easily absorb and largely nullify Lean management?
3. How does Toyota's management system avoid being influenced and nullified by classical management?

Answering the first question will provide additional evidence in support of the findings presented in "The Transformation of Lean: A Social Theory of the Lean Movement" (see Appendix II). Answering the second question will expand the understanding of how classical management and its traditions debilitate or eviscerate Lean management. It will also provide further evidence in support previous research examining why leaders resist or reject Lean management. Answering the third question will reveal the features of progressive management system design that resist the incursion of classical management.

What is Lean Management?

In this work and Appendix II, Lean management is understood to be that which has been described by James Womack and Daniel Jones in various books (Womack *et al.*, 1990; Womack and Jones, 1996, 2005) and web sites (LEI, 2020; LEA, 2020; LGN, 2020; PL, 2020). Lean is not taken to be the same as Toyota's management system (TMS), though there are many similarities (see Note 1). Instead, Lean management is understood to be a derivative interpretation of Toyota's production system (TPS) and their overall management system (Monden, 1983, Ohno, 1988; Liker, 2004). As such, Lean is incomplete in its expression of the purposes, mindsets, and practices of TMS. Yet, it is described sufficiently such that organizations, with thoughtful study and practice and the engagement of senior managers, should be able to achieve significant improvements in business performance and human resource development and capability-building.

Lean management is the popularized form of Toyota's management system that commonly exists in some form or another business enterprise post-1988 through to today. In most cases, Lean management has been narrowed in scope, bureaucratized, and handicapped in numerous ways such that the management system is heavily corrupted, and results achieved with it are substantially below that which could be achieved. In short, Lean tools and methods are made to align with the existing framework of classical management thinking and practice in most organizations. This alignment has been remarkably consistent across organizations worldwide, suggesting that there are properties intrinsic to classical management that readily absorb and nullify the principles and practices of Lean management (see Note 2). Previous research has provided ample evidence as to why this occurs (Emiliani, 2018, 2020, 2020a).

The present work seeks to deepen the understanding of this problem by using two concepts from Western philosophy, teleology and ateleology (Introna, 1996). Both terms are defined below and analyzed in relationship to business and economics, classical management, Lean management, Toyota management practices, and the Lean movement.

The Western philosophy concepts of teleology and ateleology do not appear in Eastern philosophy (see Note 3). Nevertheless, teleology and ateleology are important for understanding differences between Lean management and Toyota's management system, and especially how Lean management is understood by business leaders who subscribe to Western economic traditions and why Lean management has been largely pushed aside and thus has failed, overall, to produce the expected results (see Note 4).

It is important to recognize that Western economic tradition dating from 17th century British moral philosophy to 18th century political economy through to the present has been globally influential for some 200 years (e.g. capitalism, free markets, etc.), with some variation from country-to-country in consideration of local values, traditions, and laws. Thus, classical management exists in nearly all corporations regardless of the type, country or origin, or indigenous social culture. Classical management is globally omnipresent.

Teleology, Classical Management, and Lean Management

The term "teleology" derives from the Greek, "telos, meaning end, goal, intrinsic purpose, outcome, or finality, while "logia" (logy) means the study of a subject. Thus, teleology is the function of something in relation to its purpose or end. An activity such as carpentry is teleological in that the end is to make something useful to humans such as a chair, where the "end" is sitting. How the chair is made

– the means (design, tools, methods, process, etc.) – is irrelevant, as are the causal relationships between steps taken to execute the means. The only thing of value, or consequence, is that the end is achieved: sitting in the chair. As such, anything that is teleological does not confront the phenomenon of change (causal sequence) and its many intricate details. The focus is ends and whether change is advantageous to it. Meaning, if change is favorable to an end, and anything unfavorable to it is disregarded, then the explanation of the phenomenon (subject under study) is teleological.

If the chair is made from a protected exotic tropical hardwood nearing extinction, that is of no concern. Likewise, if the carpenter's tools are made using slave labor somewhere in the supply chain, that is also of no concern. And if the design of the chair is stolen from someone who holds the design patent, that too is of no concern. Contributing to the extinction of a species of tree, illegal forced labor, and stealing are irrelevant. The only thing that matters is the end – sitting in a chair. That is the utility which the end provides.

In business, the end is the concern while means are incidental. Indifference to process, or method, material, or tools suggests that method, material, or tools are perfect, or close enough to perfect, that there is no need for improvement. Seen another way, the existing method, material, or tools, being perfect, cannot need anything more than minor adjustment to make that which is already perfect a tiny bit better. The connection to Lean management in terms of how it is commonly understood and practiced in organizations should be obvious. The absorption of Lean tools and methods into classical management practice means that classical management and its associated tools and methods are seen by leaders as perfect, or so close to perfect, that there is virtually no need for improvement. Nor is there a need for a management system whose basis is continuous improvement. But why is that the case? It is because the process of commerce (business) is designed to achieve an end, and classical management was designed for commerce based in large part on long-established traditions (Emiliani, 2018, 2020a). These two interrelated designs are seen by the aggregate mass of devotees as both perfect and unmatched in fulfilling the need, past, present, and future.

Commerce, the commercial process, as conceived by 17th century European moral philosophers and 18th century political economists is teleological. The end of business, commercial transaction, is gain, usually pecuniary gain, and generally some form of property that is owned. The basis for business is classical and neoclassical economics, both rooted in Natural Rights and Natural Law, which, in the context of commerce, is teleological (Veblen, 1909). Commerce has an intrinsic purpose or end that is gain. This is reflected in Adam Smith's famous book, *An Inquiry into the Nature and Causes of the Wealth of Nations* (1776). However, Smith included extensive thoughts on the perils of self-interest and the need to restrain self-interest in the pursuit of pecuniary gain such that it does not do harm to individuals or society. His message was not just economic, it was moral as well. Most CEOs would agree that the purpose of business is to make money – wealth creation – and yet confide in private that morals are a lesser consideration, changeable with the times and circumstances including local, national, or international customs. Morality in business imposes means (process) that interferes with ends. It makes the pursuit of ends less efficient. Pecuniary gain being the end, and expediency being the leader's conjuration or legerdemain, places moral (individual right and wrong) and ethical (workplace rules) concerns in abeyance (see Note 5) – but these are easily and quickly resurrected when convenient to mount defenses against criticism of pecuniary gain (BR, 2019).

Business, being teleological, has as its focus ends, not means. Therefore, processes and phenomenon of change, causality, social processes and relationships, and their many intricate details, is immaterial. In business, the end justifies the means. As a result, business leaders are fixated on expediency – the use of any means, the details of which are unimportant, so long at it achieves the end. Leaders are promiscuous when it comes to their passion for quick and easy solutions ("flavors-of-the-month") to solve the problem at hand and will make any adjustments to them (e.g. shortcuts) to achieve the desired end (gain). Synonymous with "the ends justify the means" is the phrase "business is business," which means that anything and everything will be done to achieve the end, no matter whom it harms: customers, employees, suppliers, investors, communities, competitors, and even the company itself. The end, pecuniary gain, is paramount, even if it means accumulated decisions lead to the demise of the company.

In classical management, leaders are indifferent to process. Though they may say the word "process" often and have a high-level conceptual understanding, they are unfamiliar with the details of processes. Evidence for this is abundant when leaders are shown visual representations of a process that include details such as time, quantity, number of people, etc. The common refrain is "I had no idea." This habit of mind that is indifferent to process is transmitted down the hierarchy, resulting in a chaotic environment that is seen as the normal condition associated with the pursuit of pecuniary gain. Likewise, in classical management, leaders are indifferent to improvement. Though they may say the word "improvement" or "continuous improvement" often and have a high-level conceptual understanding, they are unfamiliar with the details of how improvement is made or the conditions necessary to bring about process improvement. Classical management, aligned with the teleology of business, places no demand on leaders to comprehend means (process) or improvement. In fact, it requires them to ignore it in order to achieve the end of pecuniary gain.

While Lean management has been proven time and again to offer greater pecuniary gain as well as many other benefits (see Note 6), there is a cost to adopting Lean that most business leaders seek to evade. Recall the statement by Miner, which highlights an untenable cost (2020):

> "I spent 3 years 'selling' lean face to face with CEO's and I'm still mind boggled that my success was so low. **They want the results but when**

> **you're honest with them about *how they need to change* their own behavior they say nah, not interested.**" (bold and italics added)

Lean management forces leaders to abandon solution promiscuity, expediency, shortcuts, magical beliefs, and the like, which are prized leadership possessions. Lean management offers no motivation to give up one's rights, privileges, and symbols of status. But more importantly, Lean management forces leaders to comprehend change phenomena, causal relationships, imperfect processes, the means (methods) for doing work, and how ends are achieved. In addition to degrading leader's status (see Note 7), Lean management disrupts the teleology of both business and classical management.

Faced with the choice of abandoning classical management and the teleology of business or maintaining the status quo, the choice is obvious: status quo. Yet, there is external pressure coming from investors, current and future employees (recruiting), and from others for the company to be seen as being in step with the times. So Lean management is adopted by some top leaders, but under the usual terms: solution promiscuity, expediency, shortcuts, and the like, thereby absorbing Lean management into classical management and nullifying requirements for leaders to change as well as nullifying the pecuniary and other gains that could be achieved if Lean management was adopted in its full form. Business, being a teleological process of pecuniary gain, and classical management designed to fit that specific teleological process, successfully subverts Lean management in most organizations, despite claims made by leaders that such organizations are "Lean." Instead, what they have done is create the appearance of being Lean.

The absorption of Lean management into classical management is made easier by the teleology of business, the design of classical management to fit the teleology of business, executive education (formal learning and social learning of business affairs), training and consulting businesses selling Lean to CEOs, and the representation of Lean management in business trade books as a means for "wealth creation" (Womack and Jones, 1996, 2005). This representation of Lean management, wealth creation, fits snugly within the teleology of business and the design of classical management. Importantly, this differs from earlier representations of Lean management in business trade books, which focused on the technical aspects of progressive management practice. This repeats the history of Scientific Management, wherein early business trade books focused on the technical aspects of progressive management practice followed by more explicit appeals to leaders regarding its power to create wealth. It is true, however, that the teleology of business and the design of classical management to fit it were far more significant to the absorption of Lean management than the titles, subtitles, or content of business trade books promoting wealth creation. Many training and consulting businesses, however, in pursuit of the same pecuniary ends as their clients, played a significant, perhaps sometimes unintentional, role in contributing to the absorption of Lean management into classical management.

The teleology of business requires leaders to conform its design requirements with respect to decision-making and leadership behaviors. Some behaviors that are common among top leaders adept in classical management include:

- Hear what they want to hear
- Believe they know more than the facts
- Cannot be corrected
- Prone to give fallacious arguments
- Prone to accept fallacious arguments
- Form opinions about others that cannot be changed
- Form opinions about things that cannot be changed

These rigid, unyielding characteristics reflect extraordinary levels of faith and confidence in the combination of the economic and management systems. The pathological leadership behaviors associated with classical management, which confirm indifference to process, pass unimpeded from one generation of leader to another or they emerge spontaneously among first-time entrepreneurs. Yet there remains a persistent belief over the last century that leadership behaviors can be improved, resulting in a large training and consulting industry devoted to leadership development. These well-meaning efforts are fundamentally misdirected. The behaviors listed above, integral to forceful and courageous executive decision-making, conform to the teleology of business and the skilled practice of classical management in pursuit of pecuniary gain. They are advantageous to achieving ends and so the behaviors cannot be eradicated. Simply put, executive response is teleological, not causal, as is demanded by classical management.

The design foci of commerce and classical management are intolerant of anything that introduces inefficiencies (barriers) that impede the achievement of ends, regardless of their rationality, precision, or utility. Expediency assures that the gap between the current state and the end is as narrow as possible at all times. The introduction of that which expands the gap, either in perception or reality, are cast aside because it circumscribes the scope and magnitude of exploitation. The better the design is to achieve its end, the more useful are things which enhance goal-seeking and the less useful are that which impede goal seeking. Hence, it is difficult, if not impractical and illogical, to introduce ateleology into strongly teleological system designs.

Teleological economic and management system design relies on knowledge experts who understand the systems in relation to their purpose. This is the domain of the select few, rather than the rank and file. From their perspective, there are no viable alternatives to existing systems, given their preconceptions regarding determinism, order, predictability, and outcomes. This limits flexibility and choices and leads to an inability to adapt, but which is nonetheless seen as fertile ground for opportunity.

Companies unable to adapt to the dynamic marketplace seek to merge, acquire, or divest, or declare bankruptcy or liquidate if doing so produces the greatest returns. So rather than face the social taboo of challenging one's preconceptions (Emiliani, 2018, 2020, 2020a), the leaderly thing to do is to redouble one's commitment to the status quo and savor the ensuing admiration and enhanced status bestowed by one's peers. Whatever happens must unquestioningly converge upon and confirm teleological economic and management system design. Human and social realities below the rank of leader are inconsequential because they are not advantageous to achieving ends. In the same way and for the same reason, internal and external organizational interdependencies are inconsequential. These are inefficiencies, attention to which must be avoided.

Ateleology and Toyota Management System

"Ateleology" means an ultimate purpose, or end, that is not rigidly defined *a priori* in narrow terms such as pecuniary gain (Introna, 1996; Jones 2011). Ateleology loosely defines a non-deterministic end such as completeness, balance, and harmony – an indefinite end, one that can never be achieved. In other words, the focus of ateleology is the means, not the end. The focus is on process and causality, under the assumption that this will contribute, in a continuous and limitless way, towards the end of completeness, balance, and harmony. For business to survive, pecuniary gain is a necessity. But, the means by which pecuniary gain is achieved does not have to be teleological; it can be ateleological. An ateleological process is one that recognizes an effect and responds to its cause in ways that expand (vs. narrows) ones understating of phenomena and which seeks to maintain and improve wellness.

Unlike teleology which relies on centralized expert prediction, planning, and control in relation to achieving the end, ateleology relies on local knowledge to recognize problems and make context-driven change in an uncertain environment. Instead of the experts needed for teleological processes, ateleological processes is decentralized and relies on people at the ground level to apply principles, rules, and methods to maintain and improve the wellness of the system via processes of exploration and experimentation. Classical management, unconcerned with cause and effect, is indifferent to system wellness and problems are either ignored or attempts made to correct problems are based only on symptoms.

Toyota management practice is the reverse: causality is important to maintaining and improving the wellness of the management system and the company, as well as its stakeholders who are part of the system and its proper functioning, to enable it to efficiently satisfy the ever-changing needs of customers. Localized response to problems occurring in one's work requires curiosity (the ability to think), experimentation (trial and error and the scientific method), learning, and reflection. The result is timely and flexible adaptation to continuously changing conditions. In this construction, ateleology is dynamic whereas teleology is static, the former being better suited to the ever-changing nature of commerce despite its teleology of pecuniary gain.

How does Toyota maintain and improve the wellness of its management system and of the corporation? This is described in various documents that enumerate principles and rules for employees as well as relationship-building with stakeholders (TMC, 2001, 2020, 2020a), some of which is shown below:

Five Principles of Founder Sakichi Toyoda

- Always be faithful to your duties, thereby contributing to the company and to the overall good.
- Always be studious and creative, striving to stay ahead of the times.
- Always be practical and avoid frivolousness.
- Always strive to build a homelike atmosphere at work that is warm and friendly.
- Always have respect for spiritual matters, and remember to be grateful at all times.

These five principles, as well as the seven principles listed below, are indefinite with respect to the end: completeness, balance, and harmony, or wellness. This stems in part from the impossibility of precisely defining terms such as "faithful," "studious," "practical," etc., for all people, circumstances, or all time. The expectation is that one will strive to achieve these as circumstances dictate and as one continuously interacts within the system (principles, problems, and methods) to think, learn, reflect, and improve over time.

Guiding Principles at Toyota

1. Honor the language and spirit of the law of every country and region, and undertake open and fair business activities to be a strong corporate citizen of the world.
2. Respect the culture and customs of every country and region, and contribute to economic and social development through corporate activities in their respective communities.
3. Dedicate our business to providing clean and safe products and to enhancing the quality of life everywhere through all of our activities.
4. Create and develop advanced technologies and provide outstanding products and services that fulfill the needs of customers worldwide.
5. Foster a corporate culture that enhances both individual creativity and the value of teamwork, while honoring mutual trust and respect between labor and management.
6. Pursue growth through harmony with the global community via innovative management.
7. Work with business partners in research and manufacturing to achieve stable, long-term growth and mutual benefits, while remaining open to new partnerships.

The seven guiding principles, as well as Toyota's statement of corporate social responsibility (see Note 8), expand and clarify expectations without being overly prescriptive. Together, they point to the indefinite end of wellness for the company and its stakeholders.

Preamble of CSR Policy: Contribution Toward Sustainable Development

> We, Toyota Motor Corporation and our subsidiaries, take initiative to contribute to the harmonious and sustainable development of society and the earth through all business activities that we carry out in each country and region, based on our Guiding Principles. We comply with local, national, and international laws and regulations as well as the spirit thereof, and conduct our business operations with honesty and integrity. In order to contribute to sustainable development, we believe that management interacting with its stakeholders as described below is of considerable importance, and we will endeavor to build and maintain sound relationships with our stakeholders through open and fair communication. We expect our business partners to support this initiative and act in accordance with it.

The unachievable end – completeness, balance, and harmony – reflects the reality that business operates in the realm of society and its myriad embedded human relationships, and therefore creating a need to respect and contribute to that which gives it life and the opportunity to serve customers. The teleology of classical management views such concerns superficially as "public relations" or as the political price that business is occasionally forced to pay when certain problems arise. In addition to the above principles and CSR policy statement, Toyota employees commit to using various structured problem-finding and problem-solving methods to help maintain and improve the wellness of its management system, the corporation, and its stakeholders.

Toyota recognizes the importance of, and dependence with and between, five primary stakeholders (TMC, 2020a): customers, employees, business partners, shareholders, and global society/local communities (environment, community, social contribution). Given that Toyota has perhaps been studied more than any other corporation over the last 50 years, there is ample evidence that it substantially lives up to these words through the daily practice of their management system (e.g. Liker 2004). To be sure, there are imperfections, as words brought to life by humans are subject to common cause variation and can never reach their imagined ideals. But this differs markedly from the teleology of classical management and its polestar of individualism.

One can think of classical economics and neoclassical economics, coupled with classical management, as essentially deliberate integrated master plans (teleological), whereas Toyota's management system is more akin to "let's try it and see, and then make adjustments" (ateleological) and thus emergent. This follows the familiar form of the

Plan-Do-Check-Act (PDCA) cycle, a scientific approach to problem solving that places great value on continuous experimentation (with "plan" being more the form of ideas for improvement inspired by a problem with one's work), unlike classical management where outcomes are required to be consistent with top-level company plans developed months earlier (see Note 9). Table 1 summarizes some of the key differences between classical management teleology and Toyota Management ateleology (see Notes 10 and 11).

Lean management, being a derivate interpretation of Toyota's management system, retains only some of the ateleology of Toyota's management system. That is because Lean lacks an explicit framework and guiding principles that define the indefinite end: completeness, balance, and harmony – generally, wellness. The ateleology of Lean management would be greatly improved if its guardians adopted a similar framework of principles and policies (Emiliani, 2008, 2008a). It is unlikely that business leaders long experienced in classical management will accept this improvement to Lean management, but that is no reason to not do it. The ateleology of Lean management would be strengthened by including an explicit framework and guiding principles that defined the end as completeness, balance, and harmony (i.e. wellness).

It is very difficult to find top business leaders who are willing to understand ateleology, and many may simply be incapable given the teleology of classical management and the rigid, interconnected system of economic, social, political, historical, philosophical, business, legal, and

Table 1. Comparison of Classical Management and Toyota Management System

Attribute	Classical Management Teleology	Toyota Management Ateleology
End	Pecuniary Gain	Completeness, Balance, and Harmony (Wellness)
Design	Idealistic, Part	Naturalistic, Whole
Focus	End	Means
Designer	High-Level Expert	Ground-Level Member
Unit	Individual	Team
Problem Management	Centralized	Decentralized
Problem Focus	Symptom	Root Cause
Problem Management	Centralized	Decentralized
Problem-Solving Framework	Ad hoc, Provisional	Principles, Rules, Methods
Problem-Solving	Use/Reuse Existing Solution Set	Experimentation, Learning, Reflection
System Function	Static, Equilibrium	Dynamic Adaptation, Progress
Operation	Push	Pull
Stimulus-Response	Plan-Driven	Environment-Driven
Imprint	Exploitation	Joint Exploration
Beneficiary	External: Investors Internal: Leaders	External: Customers Internal: Team Members

Adapted from Introna, 1996 and Jones, 2011.

spiritual preconceptions that they labor under (Emiliani, 2018, 2020, 2020a). Over the last three decades, there is likely less than 1000 CEOs worldwide, perhaps only 500, who have understood and accepted the ateleology of Lean management. This result does not portend a bright future for either Lean management or the Lean movement.

Teleology and the Lean Movement

Classical management is a powerful force and efforts to thwart it almost always fail. Its teleology can easily contaminate Lean management as well as the Lean movement. Because of the difficulty in achieving Lean transformations, and the sparse number of companies that have achieved Lean transformation as defined by Womack and Jones over the last 30 years (Womack and Jones, 1996), there has been a shift in the understanding of what success means in relation to efforts to apply Lean principles and practices in organizations. This shift, which occurred in early 2016, was led by the acknowledged global leaders of the Lean movement who claimed that any outcome is a good outcome, in an apparent effort to provide relief from personal frustrations and a lack of overall success in affecting substantial change in organizations. This validation of effort was warmly received by devoted Lean followers (see Note 12).

However, in claiming that any outcome of improvement work is a good outcome, solely a good outcome, the promoters of Lean inadvertently made Lean management teleological. Recall that when change is favorable to an end (success), and anything unfavorable to it is disregarded (failure), then the phenomenon is teleological. The shift from ateleology to teleology puts Lean management in alignment with how business leaders view and define success, which is anything that leaders say it is. For decades top company leaders have claimed their Lean efforts to be successful when clear, factual evidence says otherwise (see Note 13). Now that Lean movement leaders have claimed that any outcome is a success, Lean management has been further absorbed and integrated into classical management, perhaps losing its identity as more time passes.

This is one example of how preconceptions originating in classical management can invade Lean management, often without realizing that is what is happening. Society is immersed in a social, economic, political, and historical system that favors the past, and so people can unknowingly bring elements of it into the thinking and practice of Lean management. Another example is "realizing our dreams," which is a part of the thinking associated with the Toyota Way (TMC, 2001). Realizing dreams, both as a company and as individuals, means "if you can dream it you can do it." To dream also means to think, to imagine, and have ideas about how to the solve problems that the individual or team faces in their work, and to solve the problems creatively and collaboratively. This idea is largely discounted or nullified in society generally and in classical management specifically in favor of conformance to leaders demands, which usually are not born of dreams. Employees must execute management's plan and not be concerned with dreams or how to achieve them. Classical management does not accept "dreams" as a legitimate basis for action. Simply overcome any problems that one encounters so that the end is achieved. The Lean management literature is weak in educating people on this important point.

A third example is how the Lean management literature has been weak in educating people about the time-function of improvement. In classical management, improvement is understood to be a project, with a timeline, and a budget, and management approvals, and periodic management reviews, and meeting delays due to schedule conflicts and shifting priorities. This practice is imposed onto continuous improvement activities, thus forcing employees' improvement efforts to conform to classical management. Importantly, the project duration in classical management is an artifact of secondary and higher education, wherein school assignments (projects) are given generous allocations of time for completion. Leaders view this practice as a useful way to control activities. But the result is improvement proceeds exceedingly slowly despite ever-changing conditions in competitive marketplaces that do not reward slow progress. Improvements that could be completed in a day or week are completed in weeks, months, or even longer. In Toyota's management system, improvement must occur quickly. Employees learn about dreams and their ability to quickly achieve them though training and participation in kaizen.

A fourth example is how standardized work is understood in Lean and Toyota's management system, and how it is corrupted in classical management. In the former, standardized work consists of the elements: takt time (rate of customer demand), the exact work sequence an operator performs their tasks within takt time, and standard inventory (number of parts in process to assure flow). In classical management, takt time, precise work sequence, and standard inventory are usually ignored in favor of the status quo in terms of the method of material and information processing. As a result, standard work in classical management is merely the new name for long-established work procedures or written work procedures that have been re-cast in 1920s flowchart form.

A fifth example concerns the "Respect for People" or "Respect for Humanity" pillar of the Toyota Way (TMC, 2001). This general concept has been a part of progressive management since the days of Scientific Management over 100 years ago. Lean movement leaders did not recognize it until 2008 (Emiliani, 2014, 2016), and then only in the narrow context of employees rather than all stakeholders: employees, customers, supplier, investors, and communities. This error of omission, in existence for 20 years, helped Lean management fit within the teleology of classical management, which has no similar concept. The result was a façade of Lean in most corporations and thus no modification of means to achieve the end of pecuniary gain as demanded by classical management.

A sixth example is the principles of "Lean thinking" (Womack and Jones, 1996), which are enumerated as follows: 1. Specify Value, 2. Identify the Value Stream, 3. Flow, 4. Pull, 5. Perfection. The fifth principle, "Perfection" is teleological (Chatterjee, 2015). The end, "Perfection," is inconsistent with the ateleology of the Toyota Management system and the Toyota Way pillar of "Continuous Improvement."

Thus, the Lean movement is easily contaminated by classical management through small changes such as the good-hearted efforts to praise Lean practitioners for their dedicated efforts and provide motivation for continued effort, through gaps in understanding small but important details about Lean management (dreams and the time function of improvement), through the apparently willful distortion of very important foundational elements such as standardized work, omission of a bedrock principle of progressive management practice, or ascribing a goal where none exists. These problems have proven to be very difficult to correct given the teleology of classical management, which will continue to exert its strong influence in overt and covert ways, aided by mistakes intended to help Lean practitioners cope with their difficult challenges.

Summary

This work set out to answer three questions. The first expands on one of the questions answered in "The Transformation of Lean: A Social Theory of the Lean Movement" (see Appendix II):

1. How do the staff of salaried professionals derive satisfaction from their association with

Lean management given that progress is so difficult to achieve?

The salaried professional staff derives satisfaction from Lean management more through the focus on means (ateleology) than on ends (teleology) given how its application is restricted by managers who strongly favor classical management and its continuation. Staff is engaged in problem-solving and process improvement at the local level using Lean principles, tools, and methods that result in sufficient improvement to derive satisfaction from action as well as satisfaction from accumulating knowledge wealth. This is sufficient to maintain devotion to Lean management, at least until frustration with business leaders causes them to seek a new or different course. It is not known if the rate of departure of salaried professional staff from Lean currently exceeds the rate of those are attracted to Lean. Over time, one would expect this to occur given that teleological classical management remains entrenched. This could continue well into the future despite having now exposed the numerous causes for classical management's value to leaders (Emiliani, 2020, 2020a).

The next two questions pertain to the relationship between means and ends in classical management and Lean management compared to Toyota management:

2. Why does classical management so easily absorb and largely nullify Lean management?

Classical management, as practiced by managers throughout

the hierarchy, is teleological. Its end is pecuniary gain, wherein the economic and management system is seen as perfect and not in need of real improvement. Lean management offers opportunities to make minor adjustments to improve classical management consistent with its end. Major changes are not welcomed. Well-meaning efforts by loyal and dedicated internal change agents are quashed, as described in this story (Anon., 2020):

> I have tried to champion Lean at my company for over a decade now. I have made 3 serious, strong proposals on how it could be done and what could be gained from it…. Of the 3 proposals, the 1st one was approved but then ignored and allowed to die, the 2nd one was approved but then blocked, the 3rd one was met with severe anger! I have one supporter of my ideas. I showed him how we could literally shave 90% off our process. He recommended I tone that down, no that's too much, just tell them 25%, they'll never go for that… You can explain it to them [leaders], prove it on paper and they may even believe you but STILL it doesn't fly. They just want to keep on doing what they're doing just because they can. Thanks, I think, for forcing me to accept the reality that Lean is just flat out a non-starter and will remain so for the next 200 to 300 years… I feel like a failure in Lean as a leader and as an influencer in my company. I have blamed myself. I kept thinking it was me that was deficient, unable to sell my idea. That there was something wrong with me that I needed to fix in

> order to gain credibility for my Lean ideas. I have worked my ass off to study Lean and leadership and influence and marketing to try to convince them. I have given presentations, written emails, done messaging and held meetings. I have spent my own money on educating myself and our people to the positive benefits of Lean. It was very confusing for me because there was literally no downside to my Lean proposals, only upside for everybody! Nothing I proposed cost any money either. This last attempt I made to sell them on Lean was really quite shocking. My boss yelled and cussed at me like I have never experienced before, all for trying to help. I could never for the life of me figure out how trying to help was so wrong and could generate such apathy and eventually disdain until I read your books.

This description of pain and suffering are common (see Note 14) and have been publicly ignored by Lean movement leaders for decades (though there may be private acknowledgement and anguish). Ignoring this exposes the teleology of the business of Lean management, the end of which is some form of gain, most likely pecuniary gain. It also exposes hypocrisy (a Natural Right) regarding the importance of "Respect for People" and the importance of swiftly recognizing and correcting problems. Instead of recognizing the problem and investing in studies to understand it and correct it, the simplistic ameliorative solutions have long been, and remain, to offer platitudes, encouragement, and reportage of success (see Note 15).

The final question is:

3. How does Toyota's management system avoid being influenced and nullified by classical management?

Ateleological design gains greater buy-in from employees than teleological design. In the former, employees have to comprehend their work in relation to the broader system, while in the latter leaders think and ground-level personnel execute to achieve a predetermined goal (see Note 16). Toyota's management system gives people challenges, along with principles, rules, tools, and methods, that enable them to develop their skills and capabilities as human beings. In classical management, workers are seen as instruments to achieve the end of pecuniary gain. The former is joint exploration in the milieu of business and society, while the latter is exploitation in the service of commerce. Table 1 reveal a stark contrast between Toyota's management system and classical management. Yet Toyota's management system does not survive on its own. It operates within an economic system and against a competing management system that seek conformance. The people of Toyota – the leaders, the managers, the supervisors, and the team members – must fight hard every day to keep it alive and successfully repel the intrusion of classical management teleology (Toyoda, 2020, 2020a, 2020b).

This analysis also reveals some important differences between Toyota's management system and Lean management, and how the teleology of classical management penetrated both Lean management and the Lean movement. Some of this can be corrected by Lean movement leaders, whoever they may be, or by the leaders of companies in their practice of Lean management. This would include a comprehensive framework of principles (Caux, 2020) and policies, as well as various other improvements identified herein and any improvements which readers are inspired to discover.

Notes

1. Over the decades, there has been much confusion about whether Lean management and Toyota's management system (TMS) are the same. The term "lean production" was introduced to the public in 1988 (Krafcik, 1988), where "lean" was intended as a generic term for Toyota's production system method. But, as the description of Lean was only partial, it could not be a replica of Toyota's management system. In 2007, the term "lean production" lost favor and was replaced by "Lean management." Since 1988, many gaps between Lean and TMS were not closed. Despite this inattention to detail, many people today think Lean management and TMS are synonymous terms representing the exact same ways of thinking and doing things. To understand some key differences, see "Is Lean the Same as TPS?" https://bobemiliani.com/is-lean-the-same-as-tps/

2. Classical management absorbs and largely nullifies almost any substantial change in thinking or method directed towards the improvement of leadership, management, or business processes such as Total Quality Management, Agile, OpEx, Six-Sigma, Lean Six Sigma, etc. Pecuniary gain, being the *a prior* truth of commerce, weakens or disables intrusive ateleological systems because they are seen by business leaders as ineffective or inefficient.

3. Teleology and ateleology, being absent from Eastern philosophy, do not form any basis for the philosophy, thinking, or practice of Toyota's management system.

Teleology and ateleology are foreign concepts to the Japanese way of thinking generally, and to the Toyota way of thinking specifically. Toyota's Guiding Principles and CSR Policy were crafted from a normative humanistic perspective, not from an ateleological perspective.

4. The expected result was that the leaders of thousands of corporations, being smart people as they are, would easily recognize the wide-ranging merits of Lean management and rush to transform their organizations. Logical technical arguments for transformation, along with examples of successful transformation, were seen as all that would be necessary to convince presidents and CEOs. These proved to be inadequate because the basic assumptions that were made about business, leadership, and management were incorrect (see Emiliani, 2018).

5. All large companies have ethics statements against poor treatment of suppliers, yet most large corporations treat suppliers very poorly. Likewise, there are large gaps between corporate ethics statements and how other stakeholders, such as employees and customers, are treated. The steady stream of corporate financial and other types of scandals are evidence of moral failings – Morandi bridge failure, opioid epidemic, and Wells Fargo fraud are just a few recent examples. As is the case when profitable corporations conduct elective layoffs to achieve financial targets. Evidence for the routinized abeyance or morals and ethics in pursuit of the teleological end of business is overwhelming, as is the warlike glory in individual and corporate pecuniary achievement. See the citation Caux,

2020.

6. Lean management is not all upside. It challenges people in many ways. For example, Lean places higher levels of cognitive demands on people at all levels. There is a greater need for continuous training and development of human resources. Teamwork can be more challenging than contributing individually. And there is the ever-present threat of backslide to classical management.

7. The teleology of classical management is inextricably bound with the development, maintenance, and expansion of the social status of leaders. Wealth achieved through pecuniary gain in business is held in the highest esteem (Veblen, 1899; Emiliani, 2018). It is heroic, confers the highest honors, and produces levels of social and political influence in excess of merit. As noted by Veblen (Veblen, 1909): "A wealthy person meets with more consideration and enjoys a larger measure of good repute than would fall to the share of the same person with the same habit of mind and body and the same record of good and evil deeds if he were poorer." The ateleology of Toyota's management practice has no such connection to social status. However, the same cannot be said of Lean management (see Appendix II).

8. Please read the full text of Toyota's Corporate Social Responsibility Policy, particularly the words pertaining to each stakeholder: customers, employees, business partners, shareholders, and global society/local communities (see TMC, 2020a). Note that Toyota's "Customer First"

philosophy is ateleological because it is an expression of the fundamental need to be responsive to customers when serving buyers' markets. This fundamental need is not recognized in classical management, which was designed to serve sellers' markets, and continues to function today under that antiquated assumption – though it could soon turn into a correct assumption as fewer companies gain greater market power in industries such as retail, banking, and so on.

9. Classical management is highly effective at disabling ground-level application of root cause analysis, the PDCA cycle, or the Plan-Do-Study-Adjust (PDSA) cycle as Dr. Deming insisted, and other forms of fact-finding. Emergent, fact-based understanding of phenomena contradict the valuable mythologies of leadership and management and their spiritual basis (Emiliani, 2020a).

10. Management systems are a type of information system – human information systems that operate in parallel with computer information system, and the two are sometimes integrated in useful ways. Classical management and Toyota's management function as human information system (Emiliani, 2008a) with teleological and ateleological design (Introna, 1996; Jones, 2011). Classical management's human information system design is of the form of a static master plan (teleological), while Toyota's management's human information system design is emergent and dynamic (ateleological).

11. Toyota's management system is not 100 percent, perfectly ateleological. For example, target setting (current to future state) in relation to local problem-solving is teleological. As are high-level annual business targets and planning – though these are broken down into monthly or weekly targets using policy deployment, and thus channeled into the overall ateleology. The important point is that Toyota's management system is mostly ateleological, and teleological only for the things that require it, which produces a dynamic interchange between the two that helps manage change. Ateleology results in greater buy-in among larger numbers of employees compared teleological classical management where employees feel apart from one another and the company. In contrast, classical management is mostly teleological (close to 100 percent) and has an aversion to any synthesis with ateleology. A valuable connection to make here is survival. Ateleological Toyota management system has as a prime concern the survival of the company. Teleological classical management is unconcerned with corporate survival because the end, pecuniary gain, is what matters most. How the end is achieved is immaterial; it could be by remaining independent, developing new products and services, eliminating SKUs, or via merger, acquisition, or divestiture, or bankruptcy – whichever produces the greatest return at any point in time. This suggests a different mindset with respect to risk-taking induced by a rigid interconnected system of preconceptions. Classical management being more the domain of a gambler's mentality because even losses can somehow be turned into pecuniary gain. The ateleological design of Toyota's management system, being

continuously emergent and dynamic, is much less of a gamblers' paradise. It reduces risk without sacrificing the attainment of pecuniary reward.

12. This occurred at the 2016 at the Lean Transformation Summit (Ford, 2016). Rewarding effort over outcome is reminiscent of when all elementary school children receive an award of some kind or another at the end of the school year in recognition of completing one grade. The end, in the form of acknowledgment of success, and ignoring failure, is also teleological. With respect to Lean management, successful outcomes contribute to elevating one's social status (See Appendix II) even if success was not actually achieved.

13. Empirical evidence of the practice of Lean management would include things like material and information flow, Just-in-Time, respect for people (all stakeholders), management participation in kaizen, application of Lean principles and practices to the work of managing and leadership, etc.

14. The author's experience parallels (Anon., 2020). The real and potential exposure to professional and personal harm that agents of change face was an important factor in motivating the writing of *The Triumph of Classical Management Over Lean Management* (Emiliani, 2018), *Irrational Institutions* (2020), and *Management Mysterium* (2020a). Lean practitioners needed a dispassionate, fact-based understand of what they are up against, which did not exist prior to the publication of these works.

15. Because the author's work and life are mostly ateleological, he has been able to explore diverse aspects of leadership and management practice. And, that is why the Harada Method, "A step-by-step process for setting and achieving personal goals" (https://www.amazon.com/Harada-Method-Spirit-Self-Reliance/dp/0971243603) has no truck.

16. A teleological system "...spawns many teleological subsystems to solve subproblems or shortfalls... Almost every subsystem will have a feedback mechanism to ensure that the whole process is progressively converging to the ultimate goal..." (Introna, 1996). As such, teleological systems are static technical systems whereas ateleological systems are dynamic socio-technical systems that evolve according to needs and circumstances that result in a never-ending accumulation of learning and capability-building. Teleology, being focused on the end, causes one to lose sight of the broader system, and thus its problems and the need for improvement. The result is ineffective problem-solving due to a lack of systemic thinking induced by strict controls that disable generative learning.

References

Anon. (2020), Anonymous personal communication with a manager, slightly edited for brevity, May

BR (2019), "Business Roundtable: Statement on the Purpose of a Corporation," Business Round Table, Washington, D.C. 19 August, https://opportunity.businessroundtable.org/wp-content/uploads/2020/04/BRT-Statement-on-the-Purpose-of-a-Corporation-with-Signatures-Updated-April-2020.pdf, accessed 14 May 2020.

Caux (2020), "Caux Round Table Principles for Business," Caux Round Table for Moral Capitalism, St. Paul, Minnesota, http://www.cauxroundtable.org/principles/, accessed 16 May 2020

Chatterjee, S. (2015), "Teleological Dynamics of Organizational Performance: From Process to Practice and Perfectionism," Munich Personal RePEc Archive, https://mpra.ub.uni-muenchen.de/69537/, accessed 17 May 2020

Emiliani, B. (2008), *REAL LEAN: The Keys to Sustaining Lean Management*, Volume Three, The CLBM, LLC, Wethersfield, Connectcit, Chapter 3 and Appendix II

Emiliani, B. (2008a), *REAL LEAN: Learning the Craft of Lean Management*, Volume Four, Chapter 7, pp. 67-76, The CLBM, LLC, Wethersfield, Connecticut

Emiliani, B. (2008a), "Standardized Work for Executive Leadership," *Leadership and Organizational Development Journal*, Volume 29, No. 1, 2008, pp. 24-46.

Emiliani, B. (2014), "Much Study, Little Understanding," https://bobemiliani.com/much-study-little-understanding/, 22 December, accessed 17 May 2020

Emiliani, B. (2016), "The Great Lean Mystery," https://bobemiliani.com/the-great-lean-mystery/, 16 August, accessed 17 May 2020

Emiliani, B. (2018), *The Triumph of Classical Management Over Lean Management: How Tradition Prevails and What to Do About It*, Cubic, LLC, South Kingstown, Rhode Island

Emiliani, B. (2020), *Irrational Institutions: Business, Its Leaders, and The Lean Movement*, Cubic, LLC, South Kingstown, Rhode Island

Emiliani, B. (2020a), *Management Mysterium: The Quest for Progress*, Cubic, LLC, South Kingstown, Rhode Island

Ford, C. (2016), "Live Blog - The 2016 Lean Transformation Summit, Day 2," 18 March, https://www.lean.org/LeanPost/Posting.cfm?LeanPostId=550, accessed 20 May 2020

Introna, L. (1996), "Notes on Ateleological Information Systems Development." *Information Technology & People*, Volume 9, No. 4, pp. 20-39

Jones, D.T. (2011), "An Information Systems Design Theory for E-learning," Doctoral Dissertation, Chapter 2, Australian National University, https://openresearch-repository.anu.edu.au/handle/1885/8370, accessed 14 May 2020

Krafcik, J.F. (1988), "Triumph of the Lean Production System," *Sloan Management Review*, Volume 30, No. 1, pp. 41-52

LEA (2020), The Lean Enterprise Academy, http://www.leanuk.org, accessed 14 May 2020

LEI (2020), Lean Enterprise Institute, https://www.lean.org, accessed 14 May 2020

LGN (2020), Lean Global Network, http://leanglobal.org, accessed 14 May 2020

Liker, J. (2004), *The Toyota Way*, McGraw-Hill, New York, New York

Miner, G. (2020), Comment on LinkedIn made in response to the post "Does it matter if TPS and Lean are not the same thing? It depends on what you're trying to achieve. https://lnkd.in/gzRrjz3", https://www.linkedin.com/posts/professor-bob-emiliani-660a72170_is-lean-the-same-as-tps-activity-6665199871672356864-ONZl, 13 May, accessed 13 May 2020.

Monden, Y. (1983), *Toyota Production System: Practical Approach to Production Management,* First Edition, Engineering and Management Press, Norcross, Georgia

Ohno, T. (1988), *Toyota Production System – Beyond Large-Scale Production*, Productivity Press, Portland, Oregon

PL (2020), Planet Lean: The Lean Global Network Journal, https://planet-lean.com, accessed 13 May 2020

TMC (2001), "The Toyota Way 2001," Internal Document, Global Human Resources Division, Toyota Motor Corporation, Toyota City, Japan, April

TMC (2020), "Guiding Principles at Toyota," https://global.toyota/en/company/vision-and-philosophy/guiding-principles/, accessed 13 May 2020

TMC (2020a), "CSR Policy," https://global.toyota/en/sustainability/csr/policy/, accessed 13 May 2020

Toyoda A. (2020), "What we can do now for the future – An urgent online interview with President Akio Toyoda," "Are employees 'assets' or 'costs'?," *Toyota Times*, 16 April, https://toyotatimes.jp/en/chief_editor/044.html, accessed 20 May 2020.

Toyoda, A. (2020a), "Become Strong Together (Remarks by President Akio Toyoda at Financial Results for FY2020)," *Toyota Times*, 12 May, https://toyotatimes.jp/en/inside toyota/074.html, accessed 18 May 2020.

Toyoda A. (2020b), "Akio Toyoda at the FY2020 Financial Results Press Conference: "More than learning something new, I find that I am extremely calm," Question 4. "What are the priorities that shouldn't change during a crisis?," *Toyota Times*, 12 May, https://toyotatimes.jp/en/insidetoyota/075.html, accessed 18 May 2020.

Veblen, T. (1899), *The Theory of the Leisure Class: An Economic Study of Institutions*, Macmillan Co., New York, New York

Veblen, T. (1909), "The Limitations of Marginal Utility," *Journal of Political Economy,* Volume 17, No. 9, November, pp. 620-636

Womack, J., Jones, D., and Roos, D. (1990), *The Machine that Changed the World*, Rawson Associates, New York, New York

Womack, J. and Jones, D. (1996), *Lean Thinking: Banish Waste and Create Wealth in Your Corporation: The Story of Lean Production*, Simon & Schuster, New York, New York

Womack, J. and Jones, D. (2005), *Lean Solutions: How Companies and Customers Can Create Value and Wealth Together,* Free Press, New York, New York

Appendix II

The Transformation of Lean: A Social Theory of the Lean Movement

Abstract

Examines the relationship between the accumulation of knowledge wealth about Lean management by salaried professional staff and social status and status-seeking in the Lean movement using mixed methods of exploratory, causal, descriptive, qualitative research. Knowledge wealth is a key determinant of social status within the Lean movement. Consumption of knowledge is of greater significance than the actual production of process improvements due largely to the ways in which managers limit the results that can be achieved from the application of Lean principles and practices. Research is based on observations in multiple field settings and social media over a period of more than two decades. This social theory of the Lean movement from its inception in 1988 through 2020 provides an analytical framework to understand and interpret social status phenomena in the Lean movement. As a social critique of the Lean movement, analysis and findings can be utilized as feedback for making needed improvements.

Introduction

This is a follow-on work to the books *The Triumph of Classical Management Over Lean Management*, *Irrational Institutions*, and *Management Mysterium* (Emiliani, 2018, 2020, 2020a). *Triumph of Classical Management* answered two important questions:

1. Why do most top leaders resist or reject Lean management?
2. Why do most shop and office floor workers likewise resist or reject Lean management?

Irrational Institutions, and *Management Mysterium* answered the first question from two additional perspectives: rationality and aesthetics and secular spirituality. All three books meticulously examined the "institution of leadership" – common habits of thought and action – and explained why most leaders (>99% est.) greatly prefer traditional classical management over progressive Lean management. This condition has existed since the term "lean production" first came to public attention in the fall of 1988 (Krafcik, 1988). One conclusion from the series of books was that incorrect assumptions about the interests and culture of business leaders, coupled with a lack of desire to understand the current state of leadership, led to remarkably few corporate Lean transformations and the failure to advance Lean management more broadly.

Appendix II seeks to answer a third important question regarding the staff of salaried professionals (see Notes 1 and

2) who embrace Lean management and work to advance its practice in organizations:

3. Why has Lean management had a large and enduring following among salaried professional staff when most top company leaders have little or no real interest in Lean management, thus impairing the professional staffs' abilities to practice Lean management and constraining the results that they can achieve?

Logically, salaried professional staff, jointly or severally, should have little or no interest in Lean management if their leaders have no real interest in it or if their effort to apply Lean principles and practices are thwarted by leader's continued preference for classical management and associated leadership routines. Likewise, a general disinterest in Lean management among shop and office floor workers should modulate interest in Lean among salaried professional staff.

Immense money, time, and effort go into Lean training for salaried professional staff, only for it to be poorly applied or not applied at all. Why bother learning Lean management, or affiliate, advocate, or promote it under such circumstances? What is the real or perceived benefit to salaried professional staff? These and related questions are answered by examining the phenomenon of Lean transformation and associated difficulties which prevent the change-over from classical management to Lean management, which, in turn, resulted in a *transformation of*

Lean into something other than that which was intended. In particular, the advancement in social status of salaried professional staff through the accumulation of knowledge wealth.

What is Lean Management?

Lean management is understood to be that which has been described by James Womack and Daniel Jones in various books (Womack *et al.*, 1990; Womack and Jones, 1996, 2005) and web sites (LEI, 2020; LEA, 2020; LGN, 2020; PL, 2020). Lean is not taken to be the same as Toyota's management system (TMS), though there are many similarities. Instead, Lean management is understood to be a derivate interpretation of Toyota's production system (TPS) and their overall management system (Table 1). As such, Lean is incomplete in its expression of the purposes, mindsets, and practices of TMS. Yet, it is described sufficiently such that organizations, with thoughtful study and practice and the engagement of senior managers, should be able to achieve significant improvements in business performance and human resource development and capability-building.

Lean management is the point of analysis because it is the popular form that commonly exists in business enterprise post-1988 through to today. This includes for-profit business, not-for-profit, government, and non-governmental organizations. Most commonly, Lean is perceived by employees to be a group of tools used to reduce costs and improve productivity and quality. Their

Table 1 – Lean Principles and Some Popular Lean Practices

Principles	Practices
1. Specify Value 2. Identify the Value Stream 3. Flow 4. Pull 5. Perfection	Value Stream Maps A3 Reports Gemba Walks PDCA Cycle Coaching Kata Huddle Boards

larger purpose, such as achievement of Just-in-Time material and information flows, is less recognized or understood, as is its role in developing employees' capability to recognize and quickly solve problems at their root.

In most cases, Lean management has been narrowed in purpose and scope, bureaucratized, and handicapped in numerous ways such that the results achieved are substantially below that which could be achieved. The use of Lean tools, and some elements of Lean thinking, have generally been absorbed into traditional classical management practice (Emiliani, 2018). In such organizations, which clearly constitutes the vast majority, Lean management has lost its identity and is often most recognizable as a type of decoration that produces little or no gain in improvement in teamwork, problem-solving, employee development, or business results.

TMS, being much more difficult to understand and practice, requires orders of magnitude greater learning, engagement, and devotion throughout the enterprise. There are some organizations that, commendably, have developed strong

TMS-like management systems, but who refer to it as "Lean." While the higher-fidelity forms of Lean are closer in resemblance to TMS, the vast majority of organizations practice low-fidelity forms of Lean. The many variations of Lean that exist generate confusion as to what Lean management is or is not, and such variation in practice has proven to be impossible to control. Whatever one may understand Lean management to be, the salaried professional staff has always been its greatest proponent.

Problem Statement

The research question under consideration is:

> Why has Lean management had a large and enduring following among salaried professional staff when most top company leaders have little or no real interest in Lean management, thus impairing the professional staffs' abilities to practice Lean management and constraining the results that they can achieve?

How can this unusual phenomenon be explained? Six hypotheses are presented and briefly examined to determine their validity and relative importance in relation to the problem statement.

> Hypothesis 1: The salaried professional staff is attracted to Lean management because of its ideals and the promise for better a future state.

Lean management indeed promises much across many important dimensions and its thoughtful practice can produce brilliant results. There is ample empirical evidence that proves this point, coming from organizations that have transformed from classical management to Lean management (Emiliani *et al.*, 2007; Kenney, 2010). This is surely part of Lean's attraction, which easily crosses social, political, and racial lines. While interest in Lean was predominantly white males for more than two decades, it has become more diverse in the last ten years. Hypothesis 1 is judged to be significant though not a primary explanation for the above problem statement.

> Hypothesis 2: The salaried professional staff is engaged with Lean management in the hope that Lean will one day become widely accepted by business leaders, and they will thus be ready to contribute when such a day arrives.

Preparedness for when such a day arrives is admirable. The investment of time and energy in learning Lean management is significant and could one day pay off. However, company leaders have, for centuries, sought to invest in labor-saving machinery – which is their preferred method for reducing costs and improving productivity and quality, not Lean. Nothing has yet successfully altered that view. Business leaders will continue along this traditional path, utilizing whatever tools are, or will become, available to workers to aid in the use of machine technologies. Hypothesis 2 is judged to be a secondary or lesser explanation for the above problem statement.

> Hypothesis 3: The salaried professional staff mobilized in response to corporate initiatives wherein top leaders mandated Lean management to be the corporate operating system.

Company leaders, most of whom know little about Lean management, incorrectly assume it can be mandated into existence, just as any initiative can be mandated into existence under the aegis of classical management and in the honorific tradition of top-down leadership. Knowing where one's paycheck comes from, and its importance to a life well-lived, salaried professional staff dutifully comply with such a mandate. However, their allegiance to Lean has been long-lived despite leaders' perpetual misunderstandings, and perhaps their own misunderstandings of Lean as well. This suggests the validity of Hypothesis 1 and Hypothesis 2 as significant factors in the long-lived nature of the salaried professional staff's interest in Lean management. Despite this, Hypothesis 3 is judged to be a secondary or lesser explanation for the above problem statement.

> Hypothesis 4: Lean management provides the salaried professional staff with a means for providing greater value to their employer and to remain employed.

If leaders allow salaried professional staff to apply Lean principles and practices in ways that achieve business results, then it may be true that possessing such knowledge does provide greater value to one's employer and helps ensure continued employment. However, leaders often delimit what salaried professional staff can achieve by applying Lean principles and practices, preferring instead that its practice be used to optimize existing classical management. In classical management, regular full-time employees are understood to be expendable at any time (the degree of which varies from country to country). Disrespect for people is an integral feature in classical management, not a bug. Therefore, Hypothesis 4 is judged to be a tertiary or lesser explanation for the above problem statement.

> Hypothesis 5: Lean management provides the salaried professional staff with a means for elevating one's rank and increasing one's salary.

It is true that people are promoted for doing good work in the application of Lean principles and practices – especially in companies who leaders are committed to transforming the management system from classical to Lean. However, most top company leaders do not seek Lean transformation. Instead, they simply want lower-level people to become more adept at problem-solving using Lean tools in a classical management environment. Therefore, advancement opportunities are usually limited to lower- or mid-levels, with promotion to higher levels awarded to those who better reflect the understanding and practice of classical management. Therefore, Hypothesis 5 is judged to be a tertiary or lesser explanation for the above problem statement.

> Hypothesis 6: Lean management has transformed from a technical occupation to a social avocation.

The early days of Lean management (circa 1988-2000, then known as "lean production") were marked primarily by gaining the technical skills necessary to improve material and information flow, and to a lesser extent the related teamwork and, depending upon the source of technical training, the human relation skills essential to achieving the desired business outcomes. The industrial application of Lean was mainly directed towards reducing costs and improving productivity and quality. Post-2000, the understanding and meaning of Lean became diluted and highly confused as it diffused across companies and industries, accompanied by the rapid growth of Lean consulting and training organizations offering whatever service potential clients would buy. Despite this, there remains a strong affiliation with Lean management and its many variations among salaried professional staff. Given the analysis presented for Hypotheses 3, 4, and 5, Hypothesis 6 rings truest, particularly considering Hypotheses 1 and 2. Lean has been transformed over time from a technical discipline into a social avocation with a weakened technical focus. This appears to be the result of limitations imposed by successive company leaders and Lean having been largely subsumed into classical management in most organizations.

Interest in Lean management and the Lean movement have always been strongly social-affiliative. It attracts like-minded people across a spectrum of work and educational backgrounds, though historically limited in diversity. Lean, being of great practical significance, intellectually rich, and emotionally satisfying (or frustrating), commands deep and abiding interest among its followers. They are hungry for Lean knowledge and have an insatiable appetite for more. As the saying goes, "the more you learn, the more you realize how much you don't know" – unlike classical management in which learning was concluded long ago (Emiliani, 2018).

The following section presents a social theory of the Lean movement. It begins the process of understanding why followers of the Lean movement are so numerous and enduring despite the difficulties they face and illuminates important ways in which satisfaction is found.

Social Status and Lean

Status in society is achieved by having made some noteworthy accomplishment in business, politics, sports, the arts, or other field of human endeavor. Status is conferred and legitimized when the accomplishment becomes widely recognized due to its impact on society, recognition by influencers, or through sustained dissemination across the various forms of media. Success in business, especially, generates financial wealth for its owners. Financial wealth is automatically accepted as evidence of strong personal character and virtue gained through industriousness. Having great wealth is the most conspicuous form of social status because it allows one to display their high standing in society through the consumption of goods and services that are far in excess of actual needs (Veblen, 1899). However, not everyone who attains high social standing is wealthy. Social status can also be gained by possessing knowledge, such as scientists who are prominent in their field of study but receive nothing more than remuneration from their employer. They too are regarded as having strong personal character and virtue gained through industriousness.

Whether one is wealthy or not, the desire for higher social standing compels people to emulate their betters. If the marker of social status is money, then everyday people will buy expensive clothes or cars or houses to emulate their betters and display their purchases, even though they cannot truly afford to buy such things. If, on the other hand, the marker of social status is knowledge, then people will expend resources to obtain knowledge to elevate their social status within a community where knowledge is important. The Lean movement is one such community where knowledge, especially individual knowledge, is judged to be of great importance – to a much greater extent than the amount of financial wealth one may have obtained as a result of Lean (see Notes 3 and 4). The display of knowledge is the primary determinant of one's social status in Lean-world. Therefore, knowledge wealth is the more highly accredited form of wealth, and thus stands above financial wealth.

In the early days (circa 1988-2000), Lean was treated as something special, a form of private property, owned and controlled, shared with others in measured ways at measured times, for a price which reflected marketplace demand. Lean was financial wealth expropriated from Toyota Motor Corporation, though not inconsistent with their willingness to share aspects of their progressive management system (Ohno, 1988; Liker, 2004), for the benefit of all. Over time, more and more people got into the business of Lean, for better or worse. This created an explosion of Lean knowledge that was no longer controllable and could no longer be vetted by centralized sources. The internet provided the platform for widespread sharing Lean knowledge, often at no cost. Anyone with a computer and web browser was now able to gain Lean knowledge that they could then apply on-the-job, experience the outcomes, and make appropriate changes to yield better results. Information about Lean management could now be had for high prices, low prices, and free.

People have been drawn to Lean management for manifold reasons, singly or in combination. Over time a culture of Lean evolved that prized many characteristics including:

- Process Improvement
- Elimination of Waste
- Productivity
- Cost Reduction
- Quality Improvement
- Lead-Time Reduction
- On-Time Delivery
- Material & Information Flow
- Workforce Stability
- Responsiveness
- Learning
- Teamwork
- Respect for Workers
- Purpose
- A Better Life at Work
- A Better World

Lean management seemed to attract people who liked the idea of eliminating problems from work so that the work is more reliable and predictable, and thus eliminating the chaos and repetitive problems that are inherent to classical management. The initial focus on manufacturing operations was enlarged to include service operations, followed in time by the general case of any organization and every process in every department.

The social affiliation and cultural values of the new progressive Lean management were seen, and continue to be seen, as raising one's viewpoint and thinking, and hence one's status, relative to the outdated traditions of classical management. This is opposite the social affiliation and cultural values of classical management that have long been in existence, and where business leaders remain stuck on certain required aesthetics (Emiliani, 2020) and antiquated atavistic and animistic preconceptions (Emiliani, 2020a).

There is a clear desire to enhancing one's status, and likely personal prestige as well, by knowing more about Lean management than others. However, doing useful things with that knowledge, while certainly the treasured ideal, is necessarily lower in importance because of the difficulties one encounters in trying to apply knowledge of Lean on-the-job. Restrictions by company leaders as to the nature and scope of improvement, often accompanied by bureaucratic management controls and approvals, circumscribe what is achievable. Leaders raised with classical management limit achievements to only those which support the status quo of classical management and consequently serve their own interests. Additionally, one who is aggressive at applying their Lean knowledge can run afoul of their peers and experience resentment and become ostracized – even in those organizations where senior managers profess to be in full support of Lean management.

Therefore, possessing knowledge of Lean becomes the thing of greater value for most people, a type of trophy to display in the means that are possible, within a company such as during a meeting or in a newsletter, or externally such as via social media. Collections of books and a steady diet of videos, podcasts, blogs, and other low- or no-cost media to obtain Lean knowledge is symbolic of possessing a higher learning. As are group photos posted on social media to commemorate learning (e.g. Japan study tours) or having made minor improvements in the workplace. In these forms of status seeking and emulation, value lies in the consumption of knowledge, to know what others know, rather than in the production of knowledge. Nearly 50 years after the world became aware of Toyota's production system, little new knowledge has emerged from outside of Toyota pertaining to the practice of this form of progressive management. Copying others, while intensely derided by the Lean cognoscenti, is actually *de rigueur* because original thinking is scarce. It is only the simple question of whom to copy.

Nevertheless, personal knowledge of Lean management, and disdain for classical management, generates pride and prestige, and confers respect and valor to the converted. In this way, Lean is a status-enhancing object more than it is a work improvement methodology. It does things for people that they otherwise cannot do for themselves, though higher standing does not carry forward into the world of classical management as many hoped it would. This is the result of mismatched preconceptions between Lean practitioners and top company leaders (Emiliani, 2018, 2020, 2020a).

Possessing Lean knowledge is honorific in Lean culture. This helps to drive the accumulation of credentials such as certifications, training courses, conference-going, CEUs (continuing education units), and other forms of knowledge wealth (see Note 5). Myriad Lean and Lean-related certification programs confer to participants the use of various symbols upon completion. These symbols of professional achievement are recognized as having intrinsic value as well as value in the job market. Status and respectability are gained via certificates of completion (name on a diploma) and the placement of letters after one's name (see Note 6). The accumulation of symbols of knowledge is a ubiquitous cultural trait that connotes distinctions of social rank and worth that others seek to emulate. Whether knowledge wealth is put to any practical or theoretical use is of lesser importance. What matters most is having obtained it and the ability to display it.

The consequence of focusing on the social status function of Lean management is the now-common perception that Lean offers more promise than it can deliver or has delivered. Indeed, there are precious few Lean transformations when one considers the total number of large, mid-size, and small businesses in any one country or globally. Yet, there are plentiful examples of wonderful improvements that make work better or easier. This reflects a shift in interest among both business leaders and Lean practitioners, begun some two decades ago, away from Lean transformation of the whole organization to the more basic activity of process improvement, either one-time or periodically, though rarely continuously. The improvements resulting from knowledge wealth, while useful, appear in most cases to have little impact on company financial and non-financial results. As a result, business leaders continue to rely on the classical management playbook for increasing financial (enterprise) wealth. This outcome is consistent with what one would expect given the limitations senior managers place on the outcomes that can be achieved using Lean principles and practices.

Fundamentally, producing a product or service relies on processes and procedure, and is mostly deterministic. In contrast, making money is mostly stochastic – random in its opportunism and relying heavily of expediency (classical management playbook). Top leaders are not, and perhaps unable or unwilling to be, the type of systems thinkers that Lean management requires. Executives see pieces on a chessboard to move around, expand, or eliminate as market conditions change, to realize the greatest gains in financial wealth short- or long-term. Lean people see the inner workings of each piece on the chessboard and seek to improve them individually or in some larger coordinated way to produce the desired output according to specifications and marketplace demand. It is akin to the difference between an epidemiologist, who looks at the big picture (patterns of disease in a population), and a physician who is focused on ensuring the system (body) has no problems (disease) and stays healthy. In the common understanding, the purpose of the business leader and the purpose of the process improver is seen as being different, each beholden to their own sets of interests, values, and cultural proclivities. The result is a large gap between the "institution of leadership" and the "institution of Lean" – one that has proven to be extremely difficult to close. When it does close, it is more by luck than by foresight.

The institution of Lean comprises the common habits of thought and action characteristic of those who affiliate with Lean management. The institution of Lean came into being via the business of Lean, which metes out the correct ways of thinking and the correct things to do (see Note 7). The Lean community is dominated by the ideas and values of a select few people and organizations. They represent the top of the Lean social hierarchy and whose power and influence is substantial such that their implied and explicit directives are eagerly anticipated and ravenously consumed. Giving consent affirms one's reputation and social status in the Lean community, while denying consent results in spontaneous rejection. While the fundamental intent is to train and educate people in practical problem-solving, the result is more that of an appearance of understanding. A movement professing to teach people how to think for themselves inadvertently creates its own unthinking masses, so taken with the institution of Lean that they have difficulty recognizing problems with the ideology, how it is promulgated, for what purpose, and for whose benefit. The institution of Lean, dominated by the business of Lean, has effectively contaminated people's ability to think for themselves. When Lean functions more as an aspirational reflection of one's self, it cannot unleash people's intellect to practical effect. Self-actualization is diminished or denied to many, thereby reducing the amount and quality of useful improvements.

The superior rightness of Lean breeds complacency, wherein Lean's future is now defined by its less than successful past. Overall, the institution of Lean has failed to become the collective progressive force for change in management and leadership thinking and practice. But, from the start, the task of making progress was challenged by a great and diverse range of formidable obstacles both unseen and ignored (Emiliani, 2018, 2020, 2020a). The progressive model for professional thinking and conduct becomes its own conservative force due to a loss of objectivity and unwillingness to comprehend the actual situation. Cultural obedience and social acquiescence retard the thinking and innovation necessary to move the institution of Lean beyond knowledge wealth and social status seeking. But leaders in any situation do as they almost always do, which is to ignore or obscure the facts, whether intended or not, to retain what has been gained in the hope that it will never be lost.

Summary

Appendix II sought to answer the question of why Lean management remains popular with the staff of salaried professionals when most top company leaders have little or no real interest in Lean management. It identified a *transformation of Lean* that occurred over time, from a technical discipline into a social avocation with a weakened technical focus. Gaining social status through the accumulation of knowledge wealth became the dominant, though not sole, point of interest among the salaried professional staff. Included with this is the accumulation of symbols of knowledge that distinguish in social rank and worth. Causal relationships were explored to explain the transformation of Lean, and it was found to be the result of limitations in the practice of Lean management imposed by successive generations of company leaders, including the widespread sublimation of Lean management into the practice of classical management. The consequence of this include muddled understanding of the purpose and intent of Lean management; the eager consumption of Lean knowledge, know-how, and wisdom; a low rate of production of process improvements; and the production of improvements that have little or no impact on the business or its customers. These findings illuminate numerous opportunities for improving the business of Lean and the practice of Lean management in organizations.

Notes

1. The term "salaried professional staff" means the sub-group of professional staff whose role it is, by job type or otherwise, to be engaged in the daily application of Lean principles and practices. It does not represent the entirety of salaried professional staff across all functions or disciplines in a business. The term identifies the typical locus of Lean activity in organizations that have interest in the practical application of Lean management to improve business processes.

2. The author does not exclude himself from this social critique. It pertains to all affiliated with Lean, past and present, prominent or invisible.

3. Personal wealth can come from either the application of Lean management in a business (see Emiliani *et al.*, 2007) or from the business of Lean; e.g. training and consulting services, book publishing, speaking, etc.

4. Lean aficionados are indifferent to someone who has gained wealth from Lean management, either through its application in a company or through the business of Lean. What matters most is that the person is a reliable source for high quality knowledge, know-how, and wisdom about Lean management and associated leadership routines. Knowledge possessed individually, especially by former Toyota employees (e.g. sensei) or business leaders who have successful led a Lean transformation, is held in high esteem – except sometimes when it is not. Many of the world's

foremost practitioners who possess substantial (decades-long) hands-on record of significant accomplishment in real-world business settings are barely known, if not dismissed, while others who are immeasurably under-accomplished garner large audiences. Consequently, certain people have higher social status compared to others, replete with the expected mystique and devotion. This provides further evidence that possessing Lean knowledge, or the appearance of possessing it, is the thing that is held in the highest regard. In comparison, the accumulated stock of knowledge, know-how, and wisdom of the Lean community is less valued. This may be the result of the continued absence of a common definition of Lean management, alterations and mutations of Lean principles and practices that have occurred over time, and dismemberment of the Lean management system into its component parts to aid acceptance.

5. Lean is popularly said to be a "journey." The term is more apt for describing the accumulation of knowledge wealth. However, affecting the transformation from classical management to Lean management is much greater challenge, perhaps more accurately described as "Lean mountain."

6. This could be the enduring appeal of Lean Six Sigma. It offers pathways for status-laden credentials that Lean management alone does not offer.

7. This include Lean tools and methods such as value stream maps, PDCA, gemba walks, A3 reports, leader

standard work, coaching, kata, huddle boards, etc.

References

Emiliani, B., Stec., D., Grasso, L., and Stodder, J. (2007), *Better Thinking, Better Results: Case Study and Analysis of an Enterprise-Wide Lean Transformation*, Second Edition, The CLBM, LLC, Wethersfield, Connecticut

Emiliani, B. (2018), *The Triumph of Classical Management Over Lean Management: How Tradition Prevails and What to Do About It*, Cubic, LLC, South Kingstown, Rhode Island

Emiliani, B. (2020), *Irrational Institutions: Business, Its Leaders, and The Lean Movement*, Cubic, LLC, South Kingstown, Rhode Island

Emiliani, B. (2020a), *Management Mysterium: The Quest for Progress*, Cubic, LLC, South Kingstown, Rhode Island

Kenney, C. (2010), *Transforming Health Care: Virginia Mason Medical Center's Pursuit of the Perfect Patient Experience*, CRC Press, Boca Raton, Florida

Krafcik, J.F. (1988), "Triumph of the Lean Production System," *Sloan Management Review*, Vol. 30, No. 1, pp. 41-52

LEA (2020), The Lean Enterprise Academy, http://www.leanuk.org, accessed 16 April 2020

LEI (2020), Lean Enterprise Institute, https://www.lean.org, accessed 16 April 2020

LGN (2020), Lean Global Network, http://leanglobal.org, accessed 16 April 2020

Liker, J. (2004), *The Toyota Way*, McGraw-Hill, New York, New York

Ohno, T. (1988), *Toyota Production System – Beyond Large-Scale Production*, Productivity Press, Portland, Oregon

PL (2020), Planet Lean: The Lean Global Network Journal, https://planet-lean.com, accessed 17 April 2020

Veblen, T. (1899), *The Theory of the Leisure Class: An Economic Study of Institutions*, Macmillan Co., New York, New York

Womack, J., Jones, D., and Roos, D. (1990), *The Machine that Changed the World*, Rawson Associates, New York, New York

Womack, J. and Jones, D. (1996), *Lean Thinking: Banish Waste and Create Wealth in Your Corporation: The Story of Lean Production*, Simon & Schuster, New York, New York

Womack, J. and Jones, D. (2005), *Lean Solutions: How Companies and Customers Can Create Value and Wealth Together*, Free Press, New York, New York

About the Author

M.L. "Bob" Emiliani is a professor in the School of Engineering, Science, and Technology at Connecticut State University in New Britain, Connecticut, where he teaches a course on leadership, a unique course that analyzes failures in management decision-making, as well as other courses.

Bob earned a Bachelor of Science degree in mechanical engineering from the University of Miami, a Master of Science degree in chemical engineering from the University of Rhode Island, and a Doctor of Philosophy degree in Engineering from Brown University.

He worked in the consumer products and aerospace industries for 15 years, beginning as a materials engineer. He has held management positions in engineering, manufacturing, and supply chain management at Pratt & Whitney.

Bob joined academia in September 1999. While in academia, he developed the Lean teaching pedagogy and led activities to continuously improve master's degree programs.

Emiliani has authored or co-authored 23 books, four book chapters, and more than 45 peer-reviewed papers. He has received six awards for writing.

Please visit www.bobemiliani.com

Classical Management

The art of doing what is possible.

Progressive Management

The technology of doing what is impossible.

www.ingramcontent.com/pod-product-compliance
Lightning Source LLC
LaVergne TN
LVHW091042080826
845145LV00002B/591

* 9 7 8 1 7 3 2 0 1 9 1 3 3 *